Collins

D1079815

DICTIONARY OF
SCOTTISH
NAMES

HarperCollins Publishers
Westerhill Road, Bishopbriggs, Glasgow G64 2QT

The Collins website is www.collins.co.uk

This edition has been produced exclusively
for *Scotland on Sunday*

Pages 5-56 taken from *Scottish First Names*
published by Collins in 1999 © Julia Cresswell

Pages 57-96 taken from *Cool Names for Babies*
published by Collins in 2006 © Pamela Redmond Satran
and Linda Rosenkrantz

ISBN 0-00-777976-3

Printed and bound in Great Britain

Contents

Introduction   5

Scottish First Names   9

Index   54

Contemporary Names   57

The Most Popular Names in Scotland   58

Celtic Cool   59

Callum – The Top 20 of Cool   60

Sienna – Celebrity Names   62

Apple – Celebrity Baby Names   66

Sahteene – Supermodel Baby Names   82

Edmund – British Royal Names   84

Dashiell – Literary Names   86

Scottish First Names

A history of traditional Scottish names

Scotland has an unusually rich heritage of personal names, thanks to the wide variety of languages and cultures that have come together to form the nation. The earliest inhabitants of the land that we know anything about were the Picts and the British. Mystery surrounds the Picts, but it is known that they spoke a language that was one of the major branches of the Celtic languages, and was a form of the ancestor of modern Welsh, technically known as Brittonic. For simplicity I have called it British. It was probably spoken in certain areas up until the eleventh century, but had been replaced in most areas well before that. It left behind a number of personal names and many place names, some of which later became surnames, and some of these in turn were adopted as first names.

The reason the British language died out was that it was under pressure from two new waves of arriving settlers. From about the late fifth century the Scots from northern Ireland were crossing into Argyll. They spread out from this area, taking their language, the Gaelic branch of Celtic, and their stock names with them. These names form the bulk of what are considered as typical Scottish names. In the eastern Lowlands the peoples of the Anglian branch of the Anglo-Saxons were arriving, bringing with them their Germanic personal names. These were mostly made up of name elements of which any two could be recombined to make a new name. Certain elements would be traditional in certain families, so that someone's ancestry could be known by their name.

The combinations gradually became fixed into certain forms, such as Edward, that are still used today. The sixth-century British epic poem *The Gododdin* tells of the crushing defeat of the British inhabitants of Edinburgh when they tried to stop this advance. From the end of the eighth century Vikings began raids on the country, and by the middle of the ninth century the northern and western isles, Caithness and Sutherland were part of a Viking-controlled region stretching from Greenland to southern Ireland. The attraction of Scotland was its mild climate and space compared with cold, over-populated Norway. To the Vikings this was the warm south, which explains why part of their territory was named Sutherland, literally 'south land'. These Vikings spoke a language called Old Norse, which was another Germanic language. The Norse influence was long-lasting; the Hebrides, for instance, only passed from Norwegian control to Scottish control in the 1460s. Meanwhile Scandinavians and Scots had intermarried and their cultures had merged, with the result that the English form of many of the Old Norse names, for example, Sorley, come by way of Gaelic rather than directly from Old Norse.

The next big influx of names came when David I, who had been brought up in the English court, came to the throne in 1124. He brought with him a following of Norman French barons, who not only introduced French culture to the country, but also new names. These came in two forms: the names they brought over with them at the time of the Norman conquest, many of which, such as Robert, were Germanic in origin and followed the same pattern as Anglo-Saxon names; and also territorial names, such as Bruce and Lindsay, which later became first names. On top of all these influences we must add the general fund of names that came with Christianity. Additionally, though in much more recent times, there are names brought in by contact with other countries or used because they had become internationally famous and fashionable.

A peculiarity of Celtic names is that many of them have anglicized equivalents, often with no apparent connection, though sometimes there is a connection through sound and meaning. In part this is because Celtic names were felt not to be Christian names, which should be those from the Bible and saints. But more important was the pressure put on Gaelic speakers by those in power to abandon their language and culture in the hope that this would make them more amenable to their loss of freedom and status. Where possible I have recorded these anglicizations.

Another particularly Scottish naming habit is a more lavish use of surnames as first names than has been common elsewhere. While I have covered some of these in this book, it is too small to attempt to do more than deal with the most common ones. Those who wish to look further into this area should turn to David Dorward's excellent *Scottish Surnames* in the Collins Pocket Reference series. Similarly, there are many names used in Irish that are occasionally found in Gaelic-speaking areas which, again because of space, are not covered here. Those interested might refer to my Collins Gem *Irish First Names*. Those interested in looking further into Scottish names might like to start with the useful pages on the Internet sites of the General Register Office:

www.gro-scotland.gov.uk

and at their list of the current most popular names:

www.gro-scotland.gov.uk/statistics/library/pernames/index.html

For those interested in the earliest Scottish names the Internet Medieval Scotland site:

www.s-gabriel.org/names

will point you to a number of web-pages compiled by members of the Academy of St Gabriel on the subject.

Julia Cresswell

A

Adam *m*. **Adamina** *f*.

Although a biblical name, Adam has been in use among
Gaelic speakers for over a thousand years, and is still
popular today. The Gaelic spelling of the name is
Adhamh, and there is a distinctively Scottish pet form,
Adie, (Gaelic *Adaidh*), shared with AIDAN. The
Lowlands form of the name, **Edom**, is found in the
Border Ballad of *Edom O'Gordon*: 'Wha reck'd nae
sin nor shame'. There is a Scottish feminine form,
Adamina. The name **Adamnan (Adhamhnan)**,
borne by a seventh-century saint and biographer of
St Colomba, may have come from Adam, but more
probably comes from a word meaning 'fear'. It is
sometimes anglicized **Eunan**.

Aidan *m*.

This is a Gaelic name, meaning 'little fire', originally a
pet form of **Aoh** (see HUGH). It's most famous holder
was St Aidan (d.651) who left the island-monastery of
Iona to found the monastery on Lindisfarne and to
convert the pagans of Northumberia. Another earlier
Aidan, who died about 608, was king of the Dalriada
Scots. He was crowned on Iona by St Columba himself,
and thereafter fought for his kingdom's independence
from the Irish Scots. Aidan is spelt **Aodán** in Gaelic,
and can also be found in the forms **Aedan** and **Edan**
and shares the pet form **Adie**, (Gaelic *Adaidh*) with
ADAM. It is currently enjoying considerable popularity
outside its native Scotland and Ireland.

Ailsa *f.*

There have been various suggestions as to where this
name, which has been in use for over a century in
Scotland, comes from. It has been said it is a Scottish
form of Elsa, or that it represents an anglicized form
of **Ealasaid**, the Gaelic form of Elizabeth, but there can
be little doubt that most users identify it with the name
Ailsa Craig. This is a rocky island in the Clyde estuary
off the Ayrshire coast. In the island's name, Ailsa comes
from the Old Norse name which meant 'Alfsigr's
island'. The island's name reached a wide audience as
the variety name of very successful strains of tomato
and onion, and may well have been taken as a personal
name, as so many variety names are those of people.

Alan *m.*

Alan (Gaelic *Ailean*) is a Celtic name of uncertain
origin and meaning. Although it is found in all the
Celtic-speaking areas, it seems to have come initially
from Brittany, and to have spread to the other countries
by way of the Bretons who joined the Norman invasion
of England. It was certainly known in Scotland in the
eleventh century, when Walter fitzAlan, founder of the
STUART line, was one of the Normans who accompanied
King David I on his return to Scotland from England.
Alan became so well-established a name that Robert
Louis Stevenson could use the name in *Kidnapped* for
his stereotypical quixotic Highlander, Alan Breck (There
really was an Alan Breck Stewart who fought for Bonnie
Prince Charlie in the Stewarts of Appin regiment, and
escaped to France after Culloden. 'Breck' is a nickname
meaning 'freckled'.) Scottish examples of the form
ALLAN are found in Allan Ramsay (1713–1784), the
portrait painter and Allan Pinkerton (1819–1884) the

Scottish émigré who founded the Pinkerton Detective Agency in the USA. The feminine form **Alan(n)a** is not a Highland name, but a recent invention

Alexander *m.*

The ancient Greek name Alexander, 'defender of men', came to Scotland in the eleventh century, with the birth to Malcolm Canmore and St MARGARET of their fourth son, who reigned as King of Scots from 1107–24. He and his co-regent DAVID were the first kings to have non-Scottish names, and it has been suggested that Alexander was given his name by his mother who, although a descendant of the pre-Norman Conquest English kings, had been brought up in Hungary, where the medieval romances based on the life of Alexander the Great were very popular. Another Alexander, Alexander I's grandson, ruled 1214–49, and was followed by Alexander III (1249–86), giving a period of over 70 years with an Alexander on the throne, so it is hardly surprising that Alexander became a well-established Scottish name. **Sandy** (Gaelic *Sandaidh*) was the standard pet form of the name, although it could also be shortened to **Sawn(e)y** (as in the notorious fourteenth-century robber and cannibal Sawney Bean). **Saunders**, occasionally found as a first name, is usually a re-use as a first name of a surname, but was originally another pet form. **Allie** and **Al(l)y** are now common short forms. In Gaelic Alexander became **Alistair** (also **Alasdair, Alastair, Alaster, Alister**), shortened to **Alick** (Gaelic *Ailig*) and **Alec**. Feminine forms of Alexander are now so common world wide that it is difficult to distinguish which ones are particularly Scottish, but unusual feminine forms found in Scotland include **Alexina, Alickina** and **Alina**.

Alpin *m.*

Alpin (Gaelic *Ailpein*) or Alpine was the name of a
number of Pictish kings, but is best known today from
the surname MacAlpine. It's most famous bearer was
Kenneth MacAlpin ('son of Alpin'), king of the
Dalriada Scots who conquered the Picts and made
himself king of all the lands north of the Forth in
843, thus laying the foundations of what became the
kingdom of Scotland.

Andrew *m.*

As the patron saint of Scotland, St Andrew's name
has long been popular, and is still very much so today.
Dand, Dandy or **Dandie** are Scottish short forms of
the name, and **Drew** is also used. **Aindrea** and **An(n)dra**
are Gaelic forms of Andrew, which has developed into
the surname and first name Gillanders, 'servant of (St)
Andrew', from the Gaelic *Gille Ainndreis* or *Gille
Anndrais*.

Angus *m.*

Angus (Gaelic *Aonghus* or *Aonghas*) is an ancient Celtic
name meaning 'unique choice one', and was originally
the name of one of the Irish pagan gods. It is one of
the earliest Gaelic names in Scotland for, according to
tradition, the brothers FERGUS, Angus and LORNE were
Scots who settled in Dalriada (roughly the part of the
Scottish mainland nearest Ireland) about 500 AD. The
Gaelic pronunciation of the name has also appeared in
the form **Innes**, and this pronunciation explains why
the names was 'translated' by the classical name **Aeneas**
(sometimes spelt **Eneas**). The feminine forms
Angustina and **Angusina** have been recorded.

Annabel *f*.

Annabel is now so widely found in the English-speaking world that it is difficult to remember that it was once confined to Scotland. Its history is not clear, but since it was in use by the twelfth century, when Anne was not used as a first name, it does not appear to have developed from it. It is probably a variant of **Amabel**, from the Latin *amabilis* 'loveable', which elsewhere developed into Mable. It is sometimes used to 'translate' **Barabal**, the Gaelic form of Barbara. **Arabel**, which also is a Scottish name, probably developed from the same name, but its history is further confused by the fact that early examples of the name, which are also found from the twelfth century, are usually spelt in forms such as *Orabilia*, or *Orable*, as if they came from the Latin *orabilis* 'easily entreated'.

Archibald *m*.

Archibald is in origin a Germanic name formed from elements meaning 'genuine' and 'bold'. It became popular in Scotland and was often shortened to **Archie, Archy, Airchie** (Gaelic *Eair(r)dsidh*) or **Baldie**, because it was used to 'translate' the Scottish name **Gillespie** (Gaelic *Gilleasbaig*), meaning 'servant or devotee of the bishop'. The reason for this is obscure. It has been suggested that Gaelic speakers would be familiar enough with English to connect the '-bald' element of the name, originally meaning 'bold', with the fact that Gaelic *gille* means not only someone dedicated to a saint or member of the church, hence servant, but also, by implication, someone with tonsured hair, hence 'bald', with a possible further connection made between 'arch–bishop' and the Gaelic for 'bishop' for the first part of the 'translation'. Readers are free to draw their own conclusions.

Athol *m*.

Athol (sometimes **Atholl**) is a first name which comes from a place name in Perthshire. The original form of the name Gaelic *ath Fodla* means 'new Ireland', a grandiose name which would have been given to the place by early Irish settlers, although in legend the name has an even grander origin, Fodla being one of the names (all linked to placenames) ascribed to the seven sons of Cruithne (the Gaelic form of the word 'Pict') who heads the traditional list of Pictish kings.

Aulay *m*.

Aulay (Gaelic *Amhla(i)dh*) is the Gaelic form of the Scandinavian name Olaf (also the source of the name Oliver), which was introduced into the Hebrides by Viking settlers.

B

Bean *m*. Beathag *f*.

Bean (Gaelic *Beathan*) comes from the Gaelic *beatha* 'life', and was the name of a Scottish saint of the eleventh century. An old name related to it was **MacBeth** 'son of life', which was used in a religious sense to mean 'chosen one'. It is now only found as a surname thanks, of course, to the notoriety of Shakespeare's protagonist. Bean was often anglicized as Benjamin, while **Beathag**, the feminine form, was for no particularly clear reason anglicized as Sophia or Rebecca. The comparative popularity of the unusual biblical name **Bethia** in Scotland in the past may have been because it was thought to echo Beathag.

Blair *m*.

This is a Scottish surname used as a first name. The surname would originally have been given to someone who lived on or by a *blar*, the Gaelic word for 'field, plain', often referring to a battle field. It is well-used by Scottish parents today.

Bonnie *f*.

Although the word 'bonnie', which means 'fair, beautiful' is thought of as a particularly Scottish word, the name is not a Scottish invention, but a recent American creation. A great deal of its popularity is due largely to its use in Margaret Mitchell's novel *Gone with the Wind* (1939). Although it was in use before then, as is shown by the name of Bonnie Parker of Bonnie and Clyde fame. **Blythe**, 'happy', which is a word often linked with bonnie in traditional verse, is occasionally found as a female name.

Brenda *f*.

This was originally a Shetland first name, probably a female version of the Scandinavian Brand, meaning 'a sword'. It came into more general use after Sir Walter Scott used it for one of the heroines of his 1821 novel *The Pirate*. In Ireland it is used as a feminine form of Brendan.

Bruce *m*.

The family of King Robert the Bruce (Robert I) probably took its name from the French village of Brix near Cherbourg. Although other places, such as Le Brus near Calvados and Briouze in Orme, have also been suggested. The first Robert Bruce was among the forces of William of Normandy when he invaded England in 1066. The second of that name was one of the Norman barons who accompanied David I to Scotland when he took the throne. The 8th holder of the name became king himself, having defeated the English at Bannockburn in 1314. The name does not seem to have been used as a first name until the twentieth century, but by mid-century it had become so popular in Australia that it became a term for an Australian male.

C

Callum *m*.

Callum or **Calum** (either spelling can be used, though Callum is perhaps marginally the more popular form of the two at the moment) is a form of the name of St Columba (521–597), whose name came from the Latin for 'dove'. The name was popular among Irish monks because it symbolized their rejection of the pagan life of strife and war for the Christian way of peace and love, which was a change Columba found difficult. After having taken part in a battle where he was badly wounded, Columba left his native land and sailed for Scotland, to be a missionary to the pagan people there. He settled on the Hebridean island of IONA, and from their his influence spread throughout Scotland. The Irish form **Colm** is occasionally found in Scotland. MALCOLM is a development of the name.

Cameron m.

Cameron is a Scottish clan and surname used as a first name. It is currently popular both in Scotland and the United States, where it is increasingly used for girls. The name is traditionally thought to have come from an ancestor who had a crooked nose, *cam sron* in Gaelic. More prosaic people have suggested that 'crooked nose' refers to some feature of the landscape, from which the clan took its name.

Campbell m.

A Scottish clan and surname, increasingly being used as a first name, from the Gaelic *cam beul*, 'crooked mouth'. According to tradition, a nickname of Gillespic O Duithne, who lived in the early thirteenth century.

Catriona f.

This form of the name Catherine, anglicized from Gaelic **Ca(i)triona**, became famous after Robert Louis Stevenson used it for Catriona Drummond, beautiful and high-spirited heroine of his 1893 novel *Catriona*, the sequel to *Kidnapped*. It is sometimes found in the form **Catrina**, either of which can be spelt with a K. Other Gaelic names from Catherine are **Ceit** (Kate) and **Ceiteag** (Katie). Catriona is quite well used in Scotland at the moment, but the Irish form Caitlin (sometimes in the form Caitlyn) is even more popular.

Clyde m.

Although not particularly common in Scotland, it is considerably more popular in the United States and West Indies. Clyde is, of course, the name of the great river that flows through Glasgow (compare KELVIN). It is a very ancient name, which was recorded in

Roman times, and probably means 'the one who cleans', perhaps a reference to the power of the water flow. It has been suggested that the name was actually that of a river goddess, worshipped locally, but this is less generally accepted than in the past.

Coll *m.*

Coll is an early Irish name meaning 'chief, high'. According to legend, it was a name shared by three brothers who lived in Scotland for some time before winning a great kingdom for themselves in Ireland. The name was popular among the McDonalds, and the surname McColl, 'son of Coll', comes from a branch of the McDonalds.

Cosmo *m.*

A name adapted from the Italian name Cosimo 'order', may seem surprising in a list of Scottish names, but it has been in use since the eighteenth century, when it was born by the 3rd duke of Gordon. He had been given the name in honour of his father's friend, Cosimo III, Grand Duke of Tuscany. The name became traditional in the Gordon family, and from there spread to other Scottish families. A famous twentieth-century holder was Cosmo Gordon Lang, Archbishop of Canterbury 1928–1942.

Craig *m.*

This Scottish word for 'crag' was first a place name that became a surname, which in turn became a first name. Its use seems to be twentieth century, and it is currently a popular name in Scotland.

D

David *m*. **Davina** *f*.

This biblical name, meaning 'beloved', became a Scottish name because it belonged to two long-reigning kings: David I (1107–1153) and David II (1328–1371). David I was also one of the greatest landholders in England, and one of the most powerful barons in the English court where he grew up. His English upbringing meant that when he came to power in Scotland he brought with him not only many Norman customs, but also a number of Norman barons such as de Bailleul, fitzAlan (whose family name was later to become Stewart or STUART from their hereditary post of King's Steward) and de Bruse (later BRUCE). All families that were later to have such an influence on both the history and the names of Scotland. The normal pet form of David in Scotland was **Davie** (or **Davy**), the form more often used for David Balfour, the priggish hero of Stevenson's *Kidnapped*; while the Gaelic form is **Daibhidh**, shortened to **Daidh** (anglicized **Day** or **Dey**) or sometimes **Dàthaidh**. There are at least four Scottish feminine forms of the name in use by the seventeenth century: **Davina** (shortened to **Vina**), **Davida** (shortened to **Vida**) and the less common **Davinia** and **Davidina**. The first two of these have enjoyed some popularity outside Scotland.

Devorgilla *f*.

This is the English and Latin form of the Gaelic name **Diorbhail** (earlier **Diorbhorguil**), also anglicized as

Dervorguilla and **Devorguilla**. The name was often 'translated' as Dorothy. The most famous holder of the name was Devorguilla of Galloway, daughter and heiress to Alan, the last Celtic Lord of Galloway, great-great granddaughter of King David I and mother of John de Balliol, King of Scots (1292–96), who was nicknamed 'Toom Tabard' (Empty Jacket) after he was stripped of his royal insignia and throne by Edward I of England. His claim to the throne came through her. Dervorguilla was the founderess of Sweetheart Abbey, Kirkcudbrightshire, and is regarded as the founderess of Balliol College, Oxford, started by her husband apparently in penance after a quarrel with the Bishop of Durham, but endowed by her. Because of her Oxford connection, the name has occasionally been used outside Scotland for the daughters of those who went to Balliol.

Donald *m.*

Donald is one of the very earliest Celtic names, a version of it being recorded as the name of a British prince on a Roman inscription of 20 AD, and forms of the name, which means 'world ruler', are found in all Celtic languages. In Gaelic the name is **Domhnall**, shortened to **Donaidh (Donnie)** or **Dolaidh (Dolly)**, while in Ireland it takes the form **Donal(l)**. In the past the name was so popular in the Highlands that it was used as a generic term for a Highlander. The great MacDonald clan, headed by the Lords of the Isles, were descendants of Donald, grandson of the twelfth-century King Somerled of the Western Isles. A large number of feminine forms of the name recorded in the Highlands, which include **Donalda, Donaldina, Donella, Donalla, Dolina, Donelle** (primarily in Ireland), with the Gaelic forms **Donna(g), Dol(l)ag** and **Doileag**.

Dougal *m*.

Dougal, **Dugal** or **Dugald** is in Gaelic **Dubhghall**
or **Dùghall**, meaning 'dark stranger'; a term originally
used of Viking invaders. It is said that it referred
specifically to Danish Vikings, while the blonder
Norwegians and Icelanders were FINGAL, 'fair strangers'.
Whatever the truth in this tradition, the name was in
early use amongst the people of mixed Gaelic and
Viking descent in the north and west of Scotland, and
soon came to be thought of as a native Gaelic name.
The Dougal who gave his name to the MacDougalls
was the eldest son of King Somerled (Sorley) of the
Isles. The name can be shortened to **Dougie**, and
unusually for a Highland name, does not seem to
have developed any feminine forms.

Douglas *m*.

The House of Douglas was one of the most prominent
in Scottish history. The family fortunes were founded
by Sir James Douglas (c. 1286–1330), known as the
Black Douglas from his dark complexion. He was a
faithful follower of the Bruce whose real-life exploits
in the War of Independence rivalled anything in heroic
fiction. In the fourteenth century the family, now
headed by an earl, was one of the greatest landowners
in southern Scotland and could raise thousands of
experienced men to fight against English border raiders,
or to indulge in some raiding themselves. The family
split into four main branches, which were often at odds
with each other. In the sixteenth century, the Earl of
Angus, head of the Red Douglases (named after a red-
haired founder) virtually held the boy-king James V
prisoner, and ruled in his name. In the same century
the surname began to be used as a first name, often for

girls, although there is also a rare feminine form
Douglasina. The name was taken by Scottish emigrants
to Canada and the USA, where it became very popular
in the earlier part of the twentieth century, often
shortened to **Doug** or **Dougie**. Ultimately, the surname
comes from a Celtic place name *dubh glas* 'black
stream', a name found in the Southern Uplands of
Scotland where the family was originally based.

Duff *m*.

The surname Duff, sometimes found as a first name,
came from the same Gaelic word *dubh*, meaning 'dark,
black', as is found in DOUGAL and DOUGLAS.

Duncan *m*.

Duncan is the anglicized form of the Gaelic name
Donnchadh, meaning 'brown warrior' (the 'brown'
probably referring to hair or skin colour). The name
is known worldwide as the name of the murdered king
in Shakespeare's *MacBeth*, but while it can be found
outside Scotland, it has never been as popular as some
other Scottish names. It is, however, still well used in
Scotland. Shakespeare's Duncan was a real eleventh-
century king, who was already king of the Strathclyde
Britons when he became the successful claimant to the
throne of his grandfather Malcolm II, ruler of the Picts,
Scots and Lothian Angles, who had died without sons
to succeed him. Duncan thus became ruler of nearly all
of modern Scotland, as well as of a large portion of
what is now England. In 1040 Duncan was defeated
and killed in battle by a rival claimant, Macbeth, who
was in turn killed, after a successful reign, by Duncan's
son Malcolm at the battle of Lumphanan in
Aberdeenshire in 1057.

E

Effie *f.*

This is a pet form of the name **Euphemia**, from the Greek meaning 'fair speech', which was used in Scotland from the twelfth century onward, and was more common there than in other countries. The reason for this was that it anglicized the Gaelic **Oighrig**, a name of uncertain meaning, possibly 'new speckled one'. Oighrig, which was also anglicized as **Erica**, also took the forms **Eithrig** and **Eiric**, and in the past also Africa and Efric. As well as appearing most frequently as **Effie, Euphemia** could also appear as **Eppie, Phemie** or even **Fanny**, as well as being spelt **Euphame**.

Eilidh *f.*

Eilidh is the Gaelic form of Helen, originally a Greek name meaning 'bright one'. It is currently the most popular Gaelic name for girls in Scotland. Most non-Gaelic speakers pronounce it to rhyme with Hayley.

Elspeth *f.*

Elspeth, also found as **Elspet**, is a Scottish form of the name Elizabeth. It is found in various forms throughout the Christian world because it was the name of the mother of John the Baptist. It comes originally from the Hebrew meaning 'God has sworn'. Elspeth is shortened to **Elsie** and **Elspie**. The Gaelic forms of the name are **Elisaid** or **Elasaid**.

Eoin *m.*

> This is a Gaelic form of the name John. It is the form
> used for saints' names, but is also used as a given name,
> when it tends to by anglicized as Jonathan. See IAIN.

Erskine *m.*

> This is a surname which is sometimes used as a first
> name. It comes from a place name near Glasgow.

Esme, Esmé(e) *m. & f.*

> The first recorded bearer of the name Esmé was Esmé
> Stewart, 6th Seigneur d'Aubigny. (1542–83). He was
> born in France of a French mother, which may explain
> his name. It comes from the French for 'esteemed' but
> was often spelt **Aymie**, or **Aimé**, as if from the French
> for 'loved' (source of the girl's name Amy). Esmé
> Stewart was a cousin and a favourite of King James VII
> who made him Duke of Lennox and Lord High
> Chamberlain of Scotland. The name spread to other
> Scottish families, and from there to general use. It is
> often spelt **Esme** without the accent. Because it looks
> like a girl's name, it is now mainly used for girls, in
> which case it can be found in the forms **Esmée**, **Esmee**
> and even **Esma**.

Etta *f.*

> Although Etta is a widely used pet form for girls' names
> ending –etta, in Scotland it has a special role as a pet
> form of Mairead (see MARGARET), which was often
> anglicized as **Marietta** or **Maretta**.

Euan *m.*

> Euan is currently the most popular spelling of the boy's
> name which comes from the Gaelic name **Eòghann**.

The spelling **Ewan** is only slightly less popular, and forms such as **Ewen**, **Euen** and even **Evan** are also found. The Irish (and Welsh) form **Owen** has recently become popular in Scotland as well. The history of the name is somewhat obscure. Not only has Euan sometimes been confused with EOIN; and been translated as HUGH, which has muddied the waters, but the origin of Eòghann is also debated. It has been claimed that it means 'son of the yew' and is a relic of ancient tree worship, or that it comes from *eoghan*, 'youth', but most commentators now accept it as a form of the name **Eugene**, meaning 'well-born, noble'.

F

Farquhar *m*.

This name, also found as a surname, comes from the Gaelic **Fearchar**, meaning 'dear man, very dear one'. A Fearchar was king of the Dalriada Scots in the seventh century. The name is used in both Ireland and Scotland, but is most common in the Highlands.

Fenella *f*.

Fenella is the anglicized spelling of the Gaelic name **Fionnghal** (Irish **Fionnuala**), 'white shoulder'. It is also found as **Finel(l)a**, **Finola** and **Fionola**, while in Ireland **Nuala** is a very popular short form. Finola MacDonnell was the Scottish mother of the Red Hugh O'Donnell, one of the most successful Irish fighters against English rule in the seventeenth century, and is said to have been the driving force behind him. Flora MacDonald who helped Bonnie Prince Charlie 'over the sea to Skye' was probably another bearer of the name, for **Flora** was the form regularly used to translate the name. She was also known as Florence MacDonald, and sometimes signed her name Florie. As a result of her fame, Flora became a popular Scottish name, with **Florrie** used as a short form, and a Gaelic spelling **Flòraidh**. The actress Fenella Fielding has made Fenella more widely known outside Scotland.

Fergus *m*.

According to legend Fergus MacErc, also known as Fergus Mor, whose name meant 'supreme choice', along with his brothers ANGUS and LORNE, led the Scots from Ireland to Dalriada, founding the Scottish kingdom there in about 500 AD. Another famous Fergus was Prince of Galloway in the twelfth century. The name takes the form **Fearghas** in Gaelic, and has the pet form **Fergie**.

Fife *m*.

Legend says that the Scottish district of Fife, which was an independent kingdom in the early Middle Ages, got its name from Fib, one of the seven sons of the Pictish king Cruithne, whose names were used in various place names throughout Scotland. The place name became a surname, and the surname in turn became an occasional first name, also found in the form **Fyfe**. Another legend, without substance, says that the surname marks a descendant of the younger son of Macduff, earl of Fife, so cruelly killed by Shakespeare's Macbeth.

Fingal *m*.

This name has been recorded from the early fourteenth century, but became famous when James Macpherson used it as the hero of his 'Ossian' poems in 1765. In 1832 the German composer Mendelssohn wrote his *Fingal's Cave* overture, inspired by Macpherson and the cave at Staffa. Macpherson's Fingal plays the part taken in Irish myth by the great hero **Finn**. **Fingall** is an alternative spelling, and the Gaelic form is **Fionnghall** meaning 'fair stranger', traditionally used to describe blond Vikings, while the dark ones were called DOUGAL. Fingal, although well known, is not a common name. However, it was the second name of Oscar Wilde.

Finlay *m*.

This is the anglicized form of the Gaelic name **Fionnlagh**, or in some dialects **Fionnla**, which comes from *fionn laoch*, 'fair hero', traditionally the name of Macbeth's father. It was a popular name, recorded from the earliest times, and also became one of the commonest Scottish surnames. **Findlay** is an old spelling, now mainly confined to the surname; **Finley** is also found.

Fiona *f*.

This name was formed from the Gaelic word *fionn*, 'fair, white'. It was used by James Macpherson in his Ossian poems, and was apparently his creation, for the -a ending is not a Gaelic one, though there are several similar ancient names. The name became popular after it was used as a pen name by William Sharp (1855–1905) for his alter ego the romantic poetess Fiona Macleod, and is still well used in Scotland as well as elsewhere.

In recent years a number of spelling variants have occurred, such as **Fionna** and **Ffyonna**.

Forbes *m*.

This is an Aberdeenshire place name, now used as a surname and first name. It comes from Old Gaelic *forbaais*, 'at the land or place'. It could be pronounced as two syllables until the beginning of the twentieth century.

Fraser *m*.

This name comes from a Norman surname first found in Scotland in the form *Frisel*, and also *de Fresel, de Friselle* and *de Freseliere*. The meaning of this name is not known. Because of a similarity of sound, the family adopted the strawberry plant, in French *fraisier* – hence **Frazier** – as its symbol, and this may have influenced the development of the modern form. The family became an exceedingly powerful and thoroughly Gaelic one. The surname became adopted as a first name, which is currently popular and also found in the alternative spelling **Frazer**.

G

Gavin *m*.

This is the Scottish form of the name more familiar to readers of Arthurian Romance as **Gawain**. In these romances Gawain is son of King Lot of Lothian, so the name has always had strong Scottish connections.

A Scottish tradition makes Gawain himself king of Galloway. The source of the names is not clear. The early Welsh name for this character is *Gwalchmai*, 'Hawk of May', but it then appears in French as *Gauvin*, which then becomes **Gawan, Gawin** and Gavin in Scotland (as in the poet Gawin or Gavin Douglas (1475–1522). Gavin is steadily popular in Scotland and is found elsewhere in the English-speaking world.

Gilchrist *m.*

The Gaelic *gille* means a youth or servant, and is the source of the modern word *gillie*. In the early Middle Ages it was often attached to holy names to form new names, indicating that the bearer was a servant or a devotee of that particular saint. Thus Gilchrist (*Gille Chriosd*) was a devotee of Christ, **Gilleonan** (*Gille Adamhnain*) a devotee of St Adamnan (see ADAM), **Gillanders** (*Gille Anndrais*) a devotee of St Andrew and **Gillean** (*Gille Eoin*) a devotee of St John (source of the surnames Gilzean and MacLean). However, **Gillespie** (*Gille Easbaig*) was literally a servant of a bishop (see ARCHIBALD) and **Gilroy** (*Gille Ruaidh*) means 'red-haired boy'.

Giles *m.*

Giles comes from the name of a Greek saint, originally called Aegidius. This name was transformed into Giles in France, where according to tradition he ended his days. He was a popular saint in Scotland, particularly in Edinburgh, where the High Kirk was dedicated to him. In the past Giles was used for both sexes, and there was a feminine form **Egidia**, which is mainly found in Scotland. This was, in fact, often a book form of the name, the name actually being pronounced 'Giles'.

The female form of the name eventually became transformed into Julia or Juliana, while in Gaelic, which has no J, the name became **Sileas** (m.) or **Silis** (f.).

Gillies *m.*

This is one of the better-used *gille* names (see GILCHRIST), coming from the Gaelic **Gille Iosa**, 'servant of Jesus'.

Glen(n) *m. & f.*

This is a common Scottish surname, but qualifies as a Scottish first name only in that the word itself is Scottish. As a first name it is used in Scotland, but is more common in the USA and Canada, where it first rose to popularity. The forms **Glenna** and **Glenne** are also used for girls.

Gordon *m.*

This is a famous and important Scottish surname, used as a first name. The surname came from a Berwickshire place name, probably from the British meaning 'spacious fort'. It was rarely used as a first name until after 1885, when the dramatic death of General Gordon at Khartoum made the name popular both in Scotland and beyond.

Graeme, Graham *m.*

Graeme is currently the most popular spelling in Scotland of the first name that comes from the surname more frequently found as Graham. Rather surprisingly, the surname comes from Lincolnshire in England, probably the place now called Grantham. William de Graham was one of the Norman lords who accompanied DAVID I to Scotland and through marriage acquired land and power in Scotland. The spelling Graeme comes from a sixteenth-century story that the origin of the name came from a mythical Grim or Gram who broke through the Antonine Wall, built by the Romans, about 420 AD The spelling **Grahame** is also occasionally found.

Grant *m*.

This is a Scottish clan name currently a popular first name in Scotland. It comes from Norman-French *le grant*, 'big (man)', which would originally have been a nickname given to someone tall.

Gregor *m*.

This is the anglicized spelling of Gaelic **Griogair**, a form of the name **Gregory**. This is ultimately a Greek name, from the word meaning 'to be watchful', but was associated with the Latin work for 'flock, herd' and taken to refer to the Christian Good Shepherd. Because of this it became a popular name for early Christians and was chosen as a name by 16 Popes and a number of early Scottish bishops. In legend the name has been confused with the supposed King Giric or Griogar, a son of Kenneth MacAlpin. He was known to Medieval Chroniclers as 'Gregory the Great' and claimed as the founder of the MacGregor clan. Gregor is currently quite a popular name in Scotland, but **Greg** is even more popular. This can be seen as a short form of Gregor, or from the surname Greg(g) or Greig, ultimately from the same source. The Norwegian composer Edvard Grieg was a descendant of a Scotsman of this name who had settled in Norway.

Griselda, Grizel *f*.

The name Griselda became a symbol of meek, patient womanhood in the Middle Ages after Boccaccio wrote the story of Patient Griselda, telling the story of a saintly woman who kept silent and obedient despite all the terrible things her husband did to her to test her. The story was translated into English by Chaucer, a poet greatly admired by Scots in the fifteenth century. In Scotland, Grizel became the standard form of the name, and was very popular. However, it is now rare.

H

Haki *m*.

Haki is an Orkney form of the Norse name Hakon. Hakon was a common name among the Norse settlers in Orkney, and was the name of one of its prominent earls, Hakon Paulsson. Haki was sometimes anglicized as **Hercules**, and this can occasionally still be found. Hercules is also said to be used for the Gaelic name **Athairne**.

Hamish *m*.

Hamish is the Anglicization of **Seumas** or **Sheumas**, the Gaelic forms of JAMES. Both Hamish and James, a biblical name of uncertain meaning and long-standing Scottish royal name, are still popular in Scotland.

Heather *f*.

As one of the plants most closely associated with

Scotland, it is not surprising that this is a popular name with parents both in Scotland and of Scottish descent. The name first came into use towards the end of the nineteenth century.

Hector *m*.

Hector, meaning 'hold fast', and the name of the great hero of Troy, has long been a popular name in Scotland, recorded as early as 1369. Much of this popularity was because it was chosen to anglicize the Gaelic name **Eachan(n)**, which means 'horseman'. A famous holder of the name was Red Hector of the Battles, chief of the Macleans in the fifteenth century. Hector was shortened to **Heckie** or **Eckie**, and a feminine form, **Hectorina**, has been recorded.

Hugh *m*.

Hugh, though not a name commonly thought of as particularly Scottish, has had an important role in Scottish naming traditions. In origin it was a Germanic name, meaning 'mind, spirit', and has been used in Scotland since at least the twelfth century. It has also been used as the English equivalent of three different Gaelic names. It was used for **Aodh** 'fire' (see AIDAN), **Eòghann** (see EUAN) and for **Uisdean(n)**, which was a North-Western Gaelic name that was an adaptation of the Norse name *Eystein*, made up of elements meaning 'always, ever' and 'stone'. **Hughie** is a traditional pet form, and there was an old feminine, **Hughina**.

Iain, Ian *m*.

Iain is the original Gaelic form and currently the more popular spelling in Scotland of the name spelt elsewhere Ian. It is the Gaelic form of John, a biblical name meaning 'the Lord is gracious'. EOIN or **Eòin** is an alternative Gaelic form of the name. The Irish form of John, Sean or Shaun is currently popular in Scotland.

I

Ina *f*.

Because of the Scottish tradition of turning men's names into women's by adding the suffix -ina, and so producing names such as Adamina, Douglasina and Murdina, Ina has a particularly important role to play in Scottish names because it was the form these names were usually shortened to.

Inga *f*.

The Scandinavian settlers in the Northern and Western Isles, brought with them, before their conversion to Christianity, the worship of the fertility god Ing, and also the use of his name in various personal names. This can still sometimes be found in Shetland, most commonly in the shortened form Inga. In the past **Ingrid** was common. **Ingeborg (Ingibjorg)** was popular in Viking times and was the name of one of the most prominent women in the Saga of the Earls of Orkney, mother to two of the most famous earls and later wife of Malcolm King of Scots and mother to King Duncan.

Iona *f*.

This is an increasingly popular girl's name, taken from the holy island of Iona in the Hebrides. It was not much used, if at all, before the twentieth century. As a place name Iona comes from its Gaelic name *I*, itself an adaptation of the Old Norse word *ey*, 'an island'. The island's name was turned into *Ioua* in Latin, which was then misread as Iona. The island played an important role in early Scottish history. It was there that St Columba (see CALLUM) came in 563 to found the monastery from which Christianity spread to Scotland, and it was the burial place of Scotland's kings.

Irvine, Irving *m.*

These names both come from Scottish surnames derived from a place in Ayreshire, which got its name from the British *ir afon*, 'green water'.

Ishbel *f.*

Ishbel and the Gaelic **Iseaba(i)l** are Scottish forms of the name Isobel, in turn a form of Elizabeth, from the Hebrew 'oath of God'. Ishbel Gordon, Lady Aberdeen (1857–1939) was a great philanthropists and campaigner for women's rights, and Ishbel was also the name given to the daughter of Ramsey MacDonald, the first Labour prime minister. **Isbel** and the Gaelic pet form **Bealeag** (Bella) are also found.

Isla *f.*

Isla is the name of a river and glen in Perthshire, but because it is also represents the normal pronunciation of the Hebridean island of **Islay**, it may in fact come from that, particularly as Islay has been used as a first name for both sexes. The 's' is in both cases silent. The actresses, Isla St Clair and Isla Blair have made it better known.

Ivar, Ivor, Iver *m*.

Ivar (Gaelic **Imhaer** or **Iomhar**) was adopted as a
Scottish personal name in those areas which came
under Norse influence. It was a popular Norse name,
coming from words meaning 'yew' and 'warrior'. A
Viking called Ivar was a leader at the sack of Dumbarton
in 870. Ivar was a popular name among the Campbells,
one of whom, in the sixteenth century, was the
progenitor of the MacIvers. It was sometimes anglicized
to **Evander**, the name of a Greek demi-god who is
supposed to have founded a city in Italy.

J

James *m*.

The name of seven Stuart kings of the Scots, the last
two were also kings of England, and of the latter's
(James II) heir James Edward Stuart, known as the Old
Pretender, was known by some as James III and VIII.
The Latin form of the name James is *Jacobus* (Jacob),
which is why the supporters of the last of the Stuart
line were known as Jacobites, and also explains why
Jacobina as well as **Jamesina** were names such
supporters gave their daughters. The Gaelic forms of
James developed into HAMISH. It has the usual short
forms in Scotland as elsewhere, with one, **Jimmy**, being
a common form of address in the Glasgow area.

Janet *f*.

Although it is now used as an independent name, Janet

was originally a Scottish pet form of Jane, the feminine form of John from the Hebrew 'the lord is gracious'. The Gaelic form of Janet is **Seonaid**, which was anglicized to **Shona**, and there is a dialect form, **Deonaid**. Although it is itself a pet form, Janet was so popular that it developed its own pet forms. **Jessie** is a common one, and **Jenny** was used for Janet long before Jennifer became popular in the twentieth century. Less common is **Jinty**.

Jean *f*.

Like JANET, Jean is a Scottish form of Jane. **Jeanie** is a pet form, as is **Jess**, and it shares **Jenny** and **Jessie** with Janet. In Gaelic Jane or Jean becomes **Sine** (anglicized as **Sheena**), Jeanie becomes **Sineag** or **Sionag**, and Jessie, **Teasag**.

Jock *m*.

Jock is a Scottish pet form of the name **John**, the equivalent of the English Jack. Although it looks a long way from John, it comes from the affectionate ending – *kin* being added to John. The 'n' then dropped out of 'Jonkin' and the whole was shortened to leave 'Jock'. John has long been a popular name in Scotland – more than one in five soldiers in the Young Pretender's army in 1745 is recorded as a John (although this would have included those that called themselves IAIN) – and even today, when the name is in decline in other English-speaking countries, it is popular in Scotland. Jock is used as term for a Highland soldier, and outside Scotland more generally for a Scotsman. It has developed new pet forms **Jockie**, **Jockey** and **Jockan**, and is spelt **Seoc** and **Seocan** in Gaelic. John and Johnny become **Seathan** and **Seonaidh** in Gaelic.

K

Keir *m*.

A Scottish surname, which came from either the British or the Gaelic word for 'fort', used as a first name, principally in honour of (James) Keir Hardie (1836–1915), founder of the Scottish Labour Party and fighter for workers' rights.

Keith *m*.

Keith is from a Scottish surname from the British word for 'a wood' which came to be used for a first name. In the middle of the twentieth century it was popular throughout the English-speaking world, but it is not as well used now.

Kelvin *m*.

Kelvin is the name of a river that runs through Glasgow. It was taken for his title by the great Scottish scientist William Thompson, Lord Kelvin (1824–1907) when he was made a baron, after whom the Kelvin temperature scale is named. It has only been used as a first name since the twentieth century.

Kenneth *m*.

Kenneth MacAlpin, king of the Dalriada Scots of Western Scotland, conquered the Picts and made himself king of all the land north of the Forth, effectively the first king of Scots, in 843. The Gaelic form of his name is **Cinaed**, meaning 'born of fire'. Another Gaelic name **Coinneach**, 'handsome, fair one',

is also anglicized as Kenneth. The name has the pet
form **Kenny**, and feminine forms **Kenna** and **Kenina**
have been recorded.

Kirsty *f*.

Also spelt **Kirstie** and in the Highlands **Chirsty**.
This is the pet form of **Kirsten** or **Kirstin**, the Scottish
form of Christine, both currently popular names with
Scottish parents. In Gaelic the name is spelt **Curstaidh**,
Ciorstiadh, **Curstag** or **Ciorstag**. The masculine form,
Christopher, has an old pet form, **Kester**.

Kyle *m*.

As a surname, which became a first name, this comes
from an area of Ayrshire named after a fifth-century
king, Coel, who is also the origin of Old King Cole
of nursery rhyme fame. The familiar use of Kyle as a
geographic term for a narrow stretch of sea comes from
a different source, the Gaelic *caol*, 'straits'. Although
Kyle is currently popular with Scottish parents, its
world-wide popularity is not a particularly Scottish
phenomenon. There is a feminine form, **Kyla**.

L

Lachlan *m*.

This is a name we owe to the Norse inhabitants of the
Western Isles, for it means 'fjord-land', i.e. Norway, and
was originally given to immigrants from there. The
Gaelic spelling is **Lachlann** or **Lachann**. It is shortened

to **Lachie**, **Lacky** and **Lack**, and in Canada **Lockie**. There is a feminine form, **Lachina**. While it is still used in Scotland, it is not particularly popular, and is more likely to be found in families of Scottish descent in Canada and particularly Australia. General Lachlan Macquaire was Governor of New South Wales 1809–21, and gave his name to the style of architecture of the period.

Leslie, Lesley *m. & f.*

This comes from a Scottish surname, which in turn comes from a region in Aberdeenshire, of uncertain meaning, but possibly from the Gaelic for 'garden of holly'. The form Lesley was used in the late eighteenth century by Robert Burns for a woman to whom he addressed some of his poems. Originally, Leslie was used for men and Lesley for women, but Lesley is now occasionally used as a masculine, while both forms, with every additional spelling imaginable, are now used for women.

Lindsay *m. & f.*

This is Scottish surname, of the earls of Crawford, which has become a first name. The first bearer of the surname was Walter de Lindsay, who was one of the Norman barons who came north with DAVID I. Although it may come from a Norman place name, it probably comes from the area around Lincoln, which ultimately goes back to a British name meaning 'the pools', which is recorded from Roman times. It came into general use as a first name in the 1930s, but is now little used for boys. As a girl's name it is found in a huge variety of spellings, including **Lindsey**, **Lynsay** and **Linzi**.

Logan *m.*

> This is a place name, from the Gaelic word for a 'little hollow', which became first a surname and then a first name.

Lorne *m.*

> A comparatively rare name, though born by the late actor Lorne Green, but an ancient one. Tradition as it that three Irish brothers, FERGUS, ANGUS and Lorne settled in Dalriada about 500 AD. **Lorna** is not a traditional Scottish feminine form but seems to have been invented by R.D. Blackmoore for his 1869 novel *Lorna Doone*.

Ludovic *m.*

> This Germanic name is still used in Scotland, where it came into use to anglicize **Maol Dòmhnaich**, 'devotee of the Lord'. The '-mhn-' part of this name is pronounced 'v' and the 'ch' as 'k', so the two names did contain the same sequence of sounds. Ludovic is shortened to **Ludo**.

M

Magnus *m.*

> The name of the great eighth-century Emperor Charlemagne is just an adaptation of the Latin form of his name *Carolus Magnus*, 'Charles the Great'. The Scandinavians adopted the 'great' part of this, and Magnus became a popular name there. They took the

name south with them when they occupied parts of Scotland. Magnus Barelegs, King of Norway ceded the Hebrides and Kintyre to the Scottish throne in 1098, having ruled them until then. In 1116 Magnus Erlendsson, Earl of Orkney was murdered by his cousin and co-ruler, praying for the souls of his killers all the while. He was canonized and the great cathedral at Kirkwall is dedicated to him. It is therefore not surprising that the name has been particularly popular in Orkney. The Gaelic form is **Mànas**.

Maisie *f*.

Maisie is a Scottish form of MARGARET, via **Marsaili** the Gaelic form of the pet form **Margery**. It is sometimes found in the form **Mysie**, and it has been suggested that **Maidie**, a name occasionally found in Scotland and Ireland, may come from it.

Malcolm *m*.

This comes from the Gaelic *Maol Coluim*, 'devotee of St Columba' (see CALLUM). It was the name of four kings, one of whom, Malcolm II, defeated the Lothian Angles in 1038. Another king, Malcolm III, known as Canmore ('big head'), was the son of DUNCAN. He defeated Macbeth in 1057, and was married to St MARGARET. **Malcolmina** and **Malina** are feminine forms.

Malvina *f*.

Also found as **Melvina** and **Malvena**, Malvina was a name invented by the Scottish poet James Macpherson (1736–96), for his Ossianic poems. These were works based on ancient material that Macpherson had gathered, and which received international acclaim

when they were published in 1760s. Macpherson
claimed they were translations of a Gaelic epic by
Ossian, warrior-poet and son of the legendary hero
FINGAL. The detection of the fact that much of the
material was Macpherson's own invention has led to
their neglect, but some of the names live on, especially
in Scandinavia, where the poems were particularly
influential. As well as Malvina, which may be based
on the Celtic for 'smooth brow', there is **Morven** (*f.*),
the name of Fingal's kingdom (modern north Argyll).
This comes from the Gaelic for 'the big gap'. **Selma**
(*f.*) was the name of Fingal's castle, and only became a
personal name because of an ambiguity in the Swedish
translation of the poems. **Morna**, 'beloved', was the
name of Fingal's mother. It has been suggested that
Malvina may be the source of the masculine name **Melvin**.

Margaret *f.*

Although it is not a particularly popular name with
Scottish parents at the moment, Margaret has a long
history of use in the country, in honour of St Margaret
(1046–93). She was a member of the deposed Anglo-
Saxon royal family of England and was very influential
in her husband's court. She never learnt Gaelic, and as a
result the court became more anglicized. It was probably
she who chose the then exotic names DAVID and
ALEXANDER for two of her sons who later became
kings. She was deeply devout and heavily influenced
the church in Scotland. In Gaelic Margaret becomes
Mairead or **Mairghead**, with pet forms **Magaidh**
(**Maggie**) and **Peigi** (**Peggy**). See also ETTA; MAISIE.

Maxwell *m.*

Maxwell, on the river Tweed, got its name from a Saxon

called Maccus who was granted the land by David I. The family that took its name from the place rose to be earls of Morton and Nithsdale, and became one of the leading Jacobite families in the area. There has recently been something of a fashion for using the surname as a first name both in North America and the UK.

Mhairi *f*.

Mhairi is the Gaelic form of the name Mary, and is currently very popular with Scottish parents. It is sometimes found as **Màiri**, and the equivalent of the pet form Molly is **Màili**. The form of the name used for the Virgin Mary is **Moire**, and from this has developed the name **Moirean**.

Morag *f*.

Morag was originally a pet form of the Gaelic name **Mór**, 'great, large'. It was popular earlier on in the twentieth century, but is less common now. It has traditionally been anglicized, for some unknown reason, as Sarah.

Muireall *f*.

This is the Gaelic form of the name, found in all the Celtic languages, meaning 'sea-bright' and is usually anglicized as **Muriel**. **Mora(i)nn** is a related name, meaning 'sea-fair'.

Mungo *m*.

Mungo, said to mean 'beloved', was the pet name of St Kentigern, the evangelist of Strathclyde and patron saint of Glasgow. He seems to have been of British descent and a younger contemporary of St Columba, but the facts of his life are swamped by legend. The name is rare, but kept alive by the fame of the eighteenth-century Scottish missionary-explorer Mungo Park.

Murdo, Murdoch *m.*

This is the anglicized spelling of the Gaelic **Murchadh**, which comes from the Gaelic *muir* 'sea'. There are short forms, **Murdy**, **Murdie** and **Murdanie**, and the feminine forms **Murdag**, **Murdann**, **Murdina**, shortened to **Dina**, have been recorded. Murdoch, Duke of Albany was regent of Scotland during part of James I captivity in England, but was beheaded by James when he returned to Scotland in 1424.

Murray *m.*

This is a common Scottish surname used as a first name. It comes from **Moray**, meaning 'sea settlement', in north-east Scotland. The earls of Moray played a prominent part in Scottish history. Thomas Randolph, Earl of Moray was the nephew of Robert Bruce, and regent to Bruce's 5-year-old son David II, when he came to the throne in 1329. The Bonnie Earl of Moray of the well-known song was a popular Protestant lord, assassinated in the reign of James VI.

N

Neil *m.*

The story of the semi-legendary Irish hero Neal or **Niall** of the Nine Hostages, emphasizes the close connections between Ireland and mainland Britain.

He was one of the most powerful Irish kings of his time, so powerful that nine other chiefs sent him hostages, but may himself had been half British. His mother was supposed to have been a British woman captured on a raid, and he himself frequently raided across the Irish sea for booty and captives to make slaves, one of whom may have been St Patrick. The name is also spelt **Neal**, and has a Scottish pet form **Neilie**, and a feminine **Neilina**. **Nigel** is also a form of Neil. For some unclear reason Latin scribes inserted a 'g' in their translations of the name into Latin, which was then retranslated back as Nigel. **Nigella** and **Nigelia** are feminine forms.

Nessa, Nessie *f*.

These are Scottish pet forms of the name Agnes (although nowadays sometimes used for Vanessa). Nessie is of course the affectionate nickname given to the Loch Ness Monster, just as MORAG is used of the similar animal said to live in Loch Mor. The name **Senga**, which had a brief flurry of popularity in Scotland in the mid-twentieth century, is said to come from Agnes spelt backwards.

Ninian *m*.

St Ninian, the meaning of whose name is not known, was a fourth-century Strathclyde Briton who converted the Picts and Britons to Christianity. He started his ministry in 397 or 389, basing it at Whithorn. Archaeologists have found the remains of what appears to be his church. There are few hard facts about Ninian, but he appears to have been the child of Christian parents, which would indicate that the area was not entirely pagan before his time. **Ringan** is an Irish corruption of the name.

R

Ranulf *m.*

This is the Scottish form of the Old Norse name *Reginulfr*, which was formed from elements meaning 'advice' and 'wolf'. It was brought to Scotland by Viking settlers.

Robert *m.*

Robert, in origin a Germanic name formed from elements meaning 'famous' and 'bright', has long been a popular Scottish name. It was the name of one of the country's most famous kings Robert the Bruce (Robert I) who ruled 1306–29. **Rab** and **Rabbie** are distinctively Scottish short forms and it becomes **Raibeart** in Gaelic. Feminine forms have included **Roberta, Robina, Roby** and **Robena**.

Rona, Rhona *f.*

The origin of this name is a bit of a mystery. It appeared in Scotland in the 1870s, and may represent a feminine form of RONALD or RONAN or a form of Ragnhild (see RONALD). However, there is also an island between Skye and the mainland called Rona, 'rough island', and given that other islands in the area have been used as first names this may been a source.

Ronald *m.*

This is the commonest form of the many names that come from the Old Norse name *Rognvald*, formed from elements meaning 'advice' and 'ruler'. In the north of

Scotland it was commonly used in the form **Ranald**, which along with Rognvald can still be found.
The Gaelic form is **Raghnall**, and this is sometimes anglicized as **Randal**, as in the ballad 'Lord Randal'. There is a Gaelic variant, **Raonull**. Ultimately, **Reginald** and **Reynold** are from the same name. There is a feminine form of Ronald, **Ronalda**, and also a related female name, the Gaelic **Raghnaid** from Old Norse *Ragnhild*, formed from elements meaning 'advice' and 'battle'. Rognvald was a popular name in Viking Scotland, being borne among others by a king of the Hebrides, and Rognvald Kali Kolsonn, Earl of Orkney, who the sagas say travelled to Jerusalem and had dealings with the emperor of Byzantium.

Ronan *m*.

This is really an Irish name, meaning 'little seal', but various Irish saints of the name have connections with Scotland, particularly a seventh-century hermit who was supposed to have been 'tormented by the evil tongues of the women' of Eoroby on the island of Lewis, and to have been taken by a whale to the island of North Rona, where he built a chapel whose ruins can still be seen. **Ronat** (**Ronnat** or **Ronait**) is an Irish feminine form of the name.

Rory *m*.

Rory or **Rorie** is the anglicized form of the Gaelic *Ruairi(dh)* or *Ruaraidh*, meaning 'red king'. The name was also anglicized as **Roderick**, and developed the feminine forms **Rodina** and **Rhoda**.

Ross *m*.

Ross is a common British place name, meaning either

'headland' or 'wood', which became both a widespread surname and a clan name. It has a long history of use as a first name both in Scotland and Ireland.

Roy *m.*

Roy comes from the Gaelic **Ruad**, meaning 'red', and was originally a nickname for someone with red hair. It gained fame as the name of Rob Roy Macgregor (1671–1734), outlaw and adventurer, and to some the Scottish Robin Hood; particularly after a romantic version of his life was published as a novel by Sir Walter Scott in 1818.

S

Scott *m.*

This is a surname used as a first name. Although it is obviously Scottish in origin, it first became popular as a first name in the USA. Influenced, at least in part, by the fame of the author F. Scott Fitzgerald. However, it has been a popular name in Scotland for some years. It is among the 10 most common Scottish surnames, and would originally have been given to a Gaelic speaker living in a non-Gaelic area. The Scots were originally a northern Irish tribe who settled in the Western part of Scotland in the Dark Ages, and whose spreading influence throughout the country can be traced in the history of the names in this book.

Sholto *m*.

> A name quietly but steadily used, particularly in the
> Douglas family. It's origin is not entirely clear, but it
> appears to come from the Gaelic *Sioltach*, meaning
> 'sower, fruitful'.

Skye *m. & f*.

> The name of the Hebredean island used as a first name,
> in the same way that IONA is. It is quite a recent
> introduction to the list of first names, but it's use has
> been growing steadily in recent years, particularly in the
> USA. It is more common for it to be used as a girl's
> name rather than a boy's. The name of the island is
> very ancient, and is recorded from Roman times. It's
> name is probably connected with the Gaelic word *sgian*,
> 'knife', best known from the *sgian-dubh*, the black knife
> worn in the stocking in full Highland dress, and may
> refer to the deep cuts in the coastline

Sorcha *f*.

> This Gaelic name, best known Ireland, but used
> in Scotland as well, comes from a word meaning
> 'brightness'. This has led to it's being anglicized
> in Scotland as Clara, which has the same meaning,
> though in Ireland it usually becomes Sarah.

Sorley *m*.

> This name can still be found in its old form **Somerled**,
> from an Old Norse nickname meaning 'summer-
> traveller' given to someone who spent his summers
> as a Viking raider. It became a popular name with
> descendants of Viking settlers, among whom was
> Somerled Lord of Argyll – or as he preferred it King of
> Morven, Lochaber, Argyll and the Southern Hebrides –

who sacked Glasgow in 1153. As the Norse settlers were absorbed into the Gaelic population the name became **Somhairle** in Gaelic. It is this form that is anglicized to **Sorley**. It has gained fame in recent years as the name of the great Gaelic poet Somhairle MacGill-Eain, or in English translation, Sorley Maclean.

Struan *m*.

This is the place name Strowan or Struan in Perthshire, used as a first name. Strowan was long the home of the chiefs of the Robertson clan, and therefore the name is particularly used by that family.

Stuart, Stewart *m*.

Walter FitzAlan, Hereditary High Steward of Scotland, also known of Walter the Steward, or Walter Stewart, married Margery, daughter of Robert Bruce. In 1333 their son, Robert, then 17, became the regent for his 10-year-old uncle, David II. On David's death Robert was then elected king as Robert II – the first Stewart king. The royal surname name did not become used as a first name until the nineteenth century. It is found in the original spelling and in the French form used by Mary Queen of Scots, Stuart. Both are popular names in Scotland at the moment, with Stuart the preferred spelling. A rarer variant is **Steuart**, and the name becomes **Stiubhart** in Gaelic.

T

Tam *m*.

This is the particularly Scottish form of Tom, well known from Burns's 'Tam o' Shanter'. In Gaelic Thomas becomes **Tòmas** or **Tàmhas**. This last form gave rise to a surname, MacThàmas, 'son of Thomas', which was anglicized as MacTavish, giving rise to the occasional use of **Tavish** as a first name. **Tòmachan** and **Tòmag** are Gaelic pet forms of Thomas.

Thora *f*.

Thora is an Old Norse name based on the Viking thunder god Thor. It was used in the Orkneys, where Thora Sumarlidi's daughter was the mother of St MAGNUS.

Torquil *m*.

The Old Norse name *Thorketill*, probably meaning 'Thor's (sacrificial) cauldron', was introduced to Scotland by the Viking settlers and became **Torcall** in Gaelic, which in turn was anglicized as Torquil. Thor was a particularly popular god. Records from Iceland show that he was not only associated with thunder, but was something of a patron god of farmers, and one of the most widely worshipped of the gods among Viking settlers. This gave rise to a number of personal names involving his name, some of which are still in occasional use. **Thurston** comes from 'Thor's stone'; **Tormod** or **Tormailt**, commonly anglicized as Norman, comes from Thor and an element meaning 'mind, courage'; **Turlough**, **Turley** or **Turloch**, in Gaelic **Teàrlach**, and familiar to readers of

T.H. White in the old Irish spelling *Toirdhealbhach*, whichs was the name of the wild hermit who told stories to Gawain, Gareth, Agravain and Mordred in Book Two of *The Once and Future King*, and is traditionally thought of as coming from Thor, although this is now doubted; **Turval** comes from a name formed from Thor and 'ruler'. Also related to Torquil is **Taskill** (Gaelic **Tasgall**) which comes from Old Norse *Asketill*, 'god's cauldron'.

W

Wallace *m.*

This is a Scottish surname which has come to be used in honour of the great Scottish patriot and warrior William Wallace (c.1270–1305). As a surname it comes from the same Old English word that is the origin of the word Welsh, which meant 'foreign', and was used to indicate the native British people that the Saxons found in the country when they arrived. William Wallace's ancestors were probably Strathclyde Britons. The alternative spelling **Wallis** is occasionally found.

Wullie *m.*

This is the distinctively Scottish pet form of William, made famous by the cartoon character Oor Wullie. He has been appearing in the *Scottish Sunday Post* since 1934, and for many he has come to represent all that is best about everyday Scottish life. William has been a popular name in Scotland since the early Middle Ages, and takes the form **Uilleam** in Gaelic.

INDEX

Aedan *see* Aidan

Aeneas *see* Angus

Ailen *see* Alan

Ailpen *see* Alpin

Aimé *see* Asme

Aindrea *see* Andrew

Airchie *see* Archibald

Alasdair, Alec, Alic(k), Alickina, Alina, Alistair *see* Alexander

Amhlaidh *see* Aulay

Aodh *see* Aidan, Hugh

Aonghas, Aonghus *see* Angus

Arabel *see* Annabel

Athairne *see* Haki

Aymie *see* Esme

Baldie *see* Archibald

Barabal *see* Annabel

Bealeag *see* Ishbel

Beathag, Beathan, Bethia *see* Bean

Blythe *see* Bonnie

Caitriona *see* Catriona

Chirsty *see* Kirsty

Cinaed *see* Kenneth

Ciorstaidh, Ciorstag, Ciorstiadh, Ciorstag *see* Kirsty

Coinneach *see* Kenneth

Colm *see* Callum

Curstaidh, Curstag *see* Kirsty

Dand, Dandie, Dandie *see* Andrew

Deonaid *see* Janet

Dina *see* Murdo

Donnchadh *see* Duncan

Drew *see* Andrew

Eachan, Eachann *see* Hector

Eairdsidh *see* Archibald

Ealasaid *see* Ailsa

Eckie *see* Hector

Edan *see* Aidan

Edmé(e) *see* Esmé

Edom *see* Adam

Egidia *see* Giles

Eneas *see* Angus

Eoghann *see* Euan

Eoin *see* Iain

Eppie, Erica *see* Effie

Eunan *see* Adam

Euphame, Euphemia *see* Effie

Evander *see* Ivar

Fanny *see* Effie

Fearghas *see* Fergus

Finella, Finola, Fionola, Fionnghal Flora, Florrie, Floraidh
   see Fenella

Gillanders, Gille Ainndreis, Gille Anndrais *see* Andrew

Gillespie, Gilleasbaig *see* Archibald

Hercules *see* Haki

Imhaer, Iomhar *see* Ivar

Innes *see* Angus

Jenny, Jess, Jessie *see* Janet, Jean

Jinty *see* Janet

Katriona, Katrina *see* Catriona

Kentigern *see* Mungo

MacBeth *see* Bean

Magaidh, Mairghead, Mairead *see* Margaret

Màili, Màiri *see* Mhairi

Maol Coluim *see* Malcolm

Maol Dòmhnaich *see* Ludovic

Maretta, Marietta *see* Etta

Marsaili *see* Maisie

Moirean *see* Mhairi

Morna, Morven *see* Malvina

Mysie *see* Maisie

Nigel, Nigelia, Nigella *see* Neil

Oighrig *see* Effie

Peigi *see* Margaret

Phemie *see* Effie

Rab, Rabbie *see* Robert

Raghnaid, Raghnall, Ranald, Randal, Raonull *see* Ronald

Raibert *see* Robert

Rhoda *see* Rory

Rhona *see* Rona

Ringan *see* Ninian

Roderick, Rodina, Ruairi(dh), Ruaraidh *see* Rory

Sandy, Sandaidh, Saunders, Sawney *see* Alexander

Seathan, Seonaidh *see* Jock

Selma *see* Malvina

Senga *see* Nessa

Seoc, Seocan *see* Jock

Seonaid *see* Janet

Seonaidh *see* Jock

Seumas *see* Hamish

Sheena *see* Jean

Sheumas *see* Hamish

Shona *see* Janet

Sileas, Silis *see* Giles

Sine, Sineag, Sionag *see* Jean

Somerled, Somhairle *see* Sorley

Tasgall, Taskill, Teàrlach *see* Torquil

Teasag *see* Jean

Tòmachan, Tòmag, Tòmas *see* Tam

Uilleam *see* Wullie

Uisdean(n) *see* Hugh

Vida, Vina *see* David, Davina

Contemporary
Names

The Most Popular Names
in Scotland

This section presents information on the most popular names given to babies in Scotland during 2005.

The table below gives the top 20 boys' and girls' birth names in 2005. Information taken from The General Register Office for Scotland, www.gro-scotland.gov.uk

	Girls		Boys
1	SOPHIE	1	LEWIS
2	EMMA	2	JACK
3	ELLIE	3	CALLUM
4	AMY	4	JAMES
5	ERIN	5	RYAN
6	LUCY	6	CAMERON
7	KATIE	7	KYLE
8	CHLOE	8	JAMIE
9	REBECCA	9	DANIEL
10	EMILY	10	MATTHEW
11	HANNAH	11	BEN
12	OLIVIA	12	LIAM
13	RACHEL	13	ADAM
14	LEAH	14	DYLAN
15	MEGAN	15	CONNOR
16	AIMEE	16	ANDREW
17	HOLLY	17	ALEXANDER
18	ABBIE	18	AIDAN
19	JESSICA	19	THOMAS
20	LAUREN	20	AIDEN

Celtic Cool

Popularity lists are crowded with Celtic names that are beginning to win widespread acceptance as cool names. A few are included above. Here are other cool Celtic choices that appear on popularity lists. For help with pronunciation of the Irish selections, go to babynamesofireland.com, where you can hear Frank McCourt, author of *Angela's Ashes*, say each name.

Girls

AINE
AISLIN
AOIBHE
AOIFE
CAOIMHE
CLODAGH
EABHA
EIMEAR
GRAINNE
MAEVE
NIAMH
ORLA
ORLAITH
ROISIN
SADHBH
SAORISE
SIOBHAN

Boys

CATHAL
CIAN/KIAN
CIARRAN
CILLIAN/KILLIAN
COLM
DAIRE
DARA/DARAGH/DARRAGH
DIARMUID
EOGHAN
EOIN
FINN
FIONN
LORCAN
NIALL
ODHRAN
OISIN
ORAN
PADRAIGH
RIAN
RONAN
RORY
TADHG

Callum
The Top 20 of Cool

What's cool and what's popular is often decidedly *not* the same thing. But as the taste for cool becomes more widespread, as offbeat names continue to supplant stalwarts such as John and Mary on the popularity lists, we are finding more crossover between those names considered cool and those that make the top of the pops.

This list is the Top 20 Cool Names drawn from the most recent compilation of 100 Most Popular Names in the UK. They're ranked in order of frequency, so that Lily is not necessarily the coolest name of the group, but it is the name given to the most girls in that year. The number in brackets indicates each name's rank on the overall popularity list.

Depending on your personal tolerance for cool, you may see the names here as either outrageous or a bit dull. In either case, for first-time parents this list may be an eye-opening look at just how popular these choices are. And for those who want to find a name that's cool without being unique or unusual or wild, the names on this list can offer a good compromise.

But cool is a subjective quality, and while we've selected 20 of what we think are the coolest names, you may find others in the larger group you consider cooler. If you want to consult the overall popularity lists for the UK as well as several other European countries and the US, one good source is the website behindthename.com.

Girls

1. **AMELIA** (14)
2. **LILY** (16)
3. **MIA** (18)
4. **MILLIE** (20)
5. **DAISY** (28)
6. **PHOEBE** (35)
7. **KEIRA** (38)
8. **POPPY** (39)
9. **ALICE** (44)
10. **SCARLETT** (47)
11. **LIBBY** (48)
12. **NIAMH** (50)
13. **MAISIE** (55)
14. **EVE** (58)
15. **ROSIE** (61)
16. **SIENNA** (69)
17. **AVA** (84)
18. **GRACIE** (87)
19. **LOLA** (93)
20. **TILLY** (95)

Boys

1. **CALLUM** (15)
2. **JAKE** (16)
3. **GEORGE** (18)
4. **ALFIE** (22)
5. **HARVEY** (27)
6. **OWEN** (36)
7. **ARCHIE** (38)
8. **LOUIS** (42)
9. **TOBY** (48)
10. **KIERAN** (49)
11. **OSCAR** (54)
12. **FINLAY** (57)
13. **RHYS** (59)
14. **MASON** (62)
15. **JOE** (63)
16. **KAI** (67)
17. **HARLEY** (72)
18. **LUCA** (83)
19. **EWAN** (89)
20. **ZAK** (99)

Sienna
Celebrity Names

A cool name seems as essential an ingredient of stardom today as a well-sculpted body and a killer smile, a fact that can hardly be lost on parents in search of a name that will help launch their child in the world. Some of these names – Keira is a notable example – are inspiring thousands of namesakes, but their real power as a group is in making parents feel that, when it comes to names, special means beautiful, talented and famous. While names of current stars are most influential, some favourites from the past – Audrey and Ava, for instance – are also proving inspirational.

ADRIEN Brody

AIDAN Quinn

ANASTACIA

ANGELINA Jolie

ASHANTI

ASHTON Kutcher

AUDREY Tatou

AVRIL Lavigne

BALTHAZAR Getty

BECK

BENICIO Del Toro

BEYONCÉ Knowles

BJORK

BLU Cantrell

BONO

BRYCE DALLAS Howard

CALISTA Flockhart

CAMERON Diaz

CATE Blanchett

CHAKA Khan

CHARLIZE Theron

CHINA Chow

CILLIAN Murphy

CLE Du Vall

CORIN Redgrave

CRISPIN Glover

CUBA Gooding, Jr

DAMIAN Lewis

DARYL Hannah

DELROY Lindo

DEMI Moore

DENZEL Washington

DERMOT Mulroney

DIVA Zappa

DJIMON Hounsou

DIDO

DONOVAN Leitch

DOUGRAY Scott

DREW Barrymore

DULE Hill

EDIE Sedgwick

ELLE Macpherson

ELMORE Leonard

EMMA Thompson

EMO Phillips

ENRIQUE Iglesias

ENYA

EVA Longoria

EWAN McGregor

FAMKE Jannsen

FARRAH Fawcett

FELICITY Huffman

GABRIEL Aubry

GISELE Bündchen

GLENN Close

GWYNETH Paltrow

HALLE Berry

HARRISON Ford

HAYDEN Christenson

HEATH Ledger
HELENA Bonham Carter
HUGH Jackman

ILEANA Douglas
IOAN Gruffudd
IONE Skye
ISLA Fisher

JADA Pinkett-Smith
JADE Jagger
JAVIER Bardem
JEMIMA Khan
JENA Malone
JOAQUIN Phoenix
ANGELINA Jolie
JOSS Stone
JUDE Law
JULIETTE Binoche

KACEY Ainsworth
KEANU Reeves
KEIRA Knightley
KIEFER Sutherland
KIKA Markham
KOO Stark
KYRA Sedgwick

LAKE Bell
LEELEE Sobieski
LEONARDO DiCaprio
LIAM Neeson
LIBERTY Ross

LIVE Schreiber
LIV Tyler
Jennifer LOVE Hewitt
LULU
MACY Gray
MAGENTA Devine
MARIAH Carey
MENA Suvari
MILLA Jovovich
MINNIE Driver
MISCHA Barton
MOBY
MOON Unit Zappa

NATALIE Portman
NEVE Campbell

OLIVIER Martinez
ORLANDO Bloom
OWEN Wilson

PARIS Hilton
PARKER Posey
PETULA Clark
PIERCE Brosnan
PINK
PORTIA de Rossi

REESE Witherspoon
RHYS Ifans
ROMOLA Garai
RONAN Keating
ROSAMUND Pike

ROSARIO Dawson
RUPERT Everett

SADE
SAFFRON Burrows
SALMA Hayek
SCARLETT Johansson

SHAKIRA
SHALOM Harlow
SIENNA Miller
SIGOURNEY Weaver
SKEET Ulrich
STELLA McCartney
STOCKARD Channing
SUMMER Phoenix
SURANNE Jones

TALISA Soto
TATUM O'Neal
TAYE Diggs
TEA Leoni
THANDIE Newton

THORA Birch
TIGER Woods
TILDA Swinton
TUPAC Shakur
TYRA Banks
TYSON Beckford

ULRIKA Jonsson
UMA Thurman

VENDELA
VENUS Williams
VIGGO Mortensen
VIN Diesel
VING Rhames
VIVICA Fox

WINONA Ryder
WYCLEF Jean

ZOOEY Deschanel

Apple
Celebrity Baby Names

Baby-naming seems to have become a competitive sport on both sides of the Big Pond. The goal: to come up with the coolest name in town – a difficult task when your colleagues' babies are named Phinnaeus (Julia Roberts' twin), Apple (Gwyneth Paltrow and Chris Martin's daughter), and Rebel (along with Racer, Rocket, Rogue and Rhiannon the children of director Robert Rodriguez).

And what are we poor mortals to do, hearing such baby names? If not follow suit by naming our own children Apple and Rogue, then at least feel inspired to be a bit more adventurous in our choices of names. Just as celebrities influence our taste in clothes and hair and make-up, so too do they give us a new template for baby-naming.

Here are the coolest celebrity baby names of recent years, the famous parents who chose them, along with our thinking on why the names belong in this category.

ALASTAIR WALLACE   *Penny Lancaster & Rod Stewart*
> The enduring singer returned to his Scottish roots for the name of his seventh child, the middle name chosen in honour of his fiancée's grandfather.

AMELIA   *Lisa Rinna & Harry Hamlin*
> A long neglected Victorian name that's a cooler, more unusual choice than the similar-in-feel but more ordinary Amanda or Emily.

ANAÏS   *Noel Gallagher*

The guiding force of Oasis undoubtedly took as his naming inspiration the famed novelist and diarist Anaïs Nin.

APPLE   *Gwyneth Paltrow & Chris Martin*

This high-profile couple made international headlines when they chose this wholesome, rosy-cheeked fruit name for their daughter, setting off shock waves, but we can see it starting a trend – with Plums, Berrys, Cherrys, and even Lemons, Mangos and Papayas possibly populating schoolrooms of the future.

ASSISI   *Jade Jagger*

Sir Mick's granddaughter was given this unique place name, evocative of the lovely Umbrian hill town, not to mention the benevolent St Francis. Her sister **AMBA**'s name is an example of an altered spelling that works.

ATLANTA NOO   *Amanda de Cadenet & John Taylor*

What's noo? Atlanta is one of the fresher sounding US place names, as are Avalon and Alabama.

AUDEN   *Noah Wyle (daughter) / Amber Valletta (son)*

This softly poetic namesake of W.H. Auden has recently become a fashionable first name option, used for both sexes: definitely a cool name to watch.

AURELIUS   *Elle Macpherson*

Given the supermodel seal of approval, this is one of the band of Roman Emperor names now in the realm of possibility.

AVA *Aidan Quinn / Heather Locklear & Richie Sambora /*
Reese Witherspoon & Ryan Philippe / John McEnroe /
Hugh Jackman / Martina McBride
One of the hottest current celebrity favourites and
racing up all popularity lists, Ava radiates the sultry retro
glamour of Ava Gardner.

BANJO PATRICK *Rachel Griffiths*
When the Oz-born actress chose this highly unusual
name for her son, many assumed it was a bizarre
invention, but it has a legitimate tie to bush poet
'Banjo' Paterson. Banjo's younger sister has another
tie to that continent, with the place name Adelaide.

BEATRICE MILLY *Heather Mills & Paul McCartney*
The christening of Princess Beatrice brought this
traditional name back into the public eye, and now it
has further exposure as a Beatle baby. It has real family
significance: Beatrice is the name of Heather's mother,
and Milly was chosen to honour Sir Paul's aunt.

BECKETT *Malcom MacDowall / Natalie Maines / Melissa*
Etheridge / Conan O'Brian
An appealing surname-name rich in literary
associations, both to the play and movie based on the
life of Saint Thomas B. and to the Irish playwright-
novelist Samuel B., it's recently become a red hot celeb
favourite.

BELLA *Eddie Murphy / Keenen Ivory Wayans / Mark Ruffalo*
Everything *ella* is stylish right now, and Bella, with its
literally beautiful meaning, is one of the less overused,
with a nice old world, grandmotherly veneer.

BETTY KITTEN *Jane Goldman & Jonathan Ross*

Could any pair of names give off a more retro-camp vibe than this? – they sound like something lifted straight out of an American sitcom of the fifties. The couple's other offspring, Honey Kinney and Harvey Kirby, have a similar feel.

BILLY RAY *Helena Bonham-Carter & Tim Burton*

This cool couple opted to put the freckle-faced nickname straight onto the birth certificate. A trend more and more parents are following, as in Alfie, Bertie, Freddie et al.

BLUEBELL MADONNA *Geri Halliwell*

Bluebell, though undeniably sweet and original, may be one of those names – much like those of fellow Spicebabies Brooklyn, Romeo, and Phoenix – that are reaching hard for cool and therefore don't achieve it.

BROOKLYN *Victoria Adams & David Beckham*

Named for the New York borough of his conception, the much-publicized first Beckham boy set off a veritable epidemic of ambi-gender Brooklyns. Brothers Romeo and Cruz could do the same.

CARYS *Catherine Zeta Jones & Michael Douglas*

Catherine Zeta Jones looked back to her Welsh roots when choosing this name, thereby giving it wider international recognition.

CASPAR *Claudia Schiffer*
German-born supermodel Schiffer took a similar path by selecting a name well used in her native country but considered pleasantly quirky in other parts of the western world. Let's hope her boy doesn't get too much Casper-the-friendly-ghost teasing.

COCO REILLY *Courtney Cox & David Arquette*
Though it has some fashion power via legendary designer Chanel, Coco, like high-kicking friends Gigi and Fifi, has a lot of Gallic spirit but is short on substance.

COSIMA *Nigella Lawson*
Elegant and exotic with classical music associations.

CRUZ *Victoria Adams & David Beckham*
Once again, the Beckhams caused quite a stir when they chose this unisex Latino surname for their third son; it packs a lot of energy and charm into its single syllable.

DAISY BOO *Jamie Oliver*
In the Top 50 names, Daisy is more hot than cool, but the playful middle name makes it stand out from the other daisies in the garden.

DASHIELL *Cate Blanchett/Lisa Rinna & Harry Hamlin/ Alice Cooper*
A lot of dash and a touch of mystery thanks to detective writer Dashiell Hammett.

DEACON   *Reese Witherspoon & Ryan Philippe*

After giving their first child the trendy name Ava, this glitzy couple sought and found something unique for their second. It links up three current trends: occupational names, religious names and interesting names from one's family history – Charles Louis 'Deacon' Philippe was a distantly related early 19th century baseball player.

DELILAH   *Lisa Rinna & Harry Hamlin*

The quintessentially seductive name. How can a Delilah not be gorgeous, and cool?

DENIM KOLE   *Toni Braxton*

Named after Denham, a character in *To Sir With Love*. But substituting K's for C's is no longer kool.

DEXTER   *Diane Keaton*

A nerdy boy's name comes alive when given to a girl, and these days every name with an x in it is cool.

DIXIE DOT   *Anna Ryder Richardson*

This style maven has chosen names for her daughters – the other is Bibi Belle – that have tons of alliterative pizzazz.

EJA   *Shania Twain*

This unusual phonetic spelling of Asia gives the name a more masculine flavour.

ELIJAH BOB PATRICUS GUGGI Q   *Bono*

Don't try this at home.

ELLERY *Laura Dern*
>Ellery has gone from middle-aged, mid-century American mystery writer/detective to hot girl's name, a trend also happening with Elliot.

ESMÉ *Tracy Pollan & Michael J. Fox/Samantha Morton/Anthony Edwards*
>A captivating JD Salinger-inspired choice.

ESTHER ROSE *Ewan McGregor*
>A perfect companion name for sister **CLARA MATHILDE**, Esther is a so-clunky-it's-fresh Old Testament name. A star's child has a head start on pulling off a name like this.

FINN *Jane Leeves/Andrea Catherwood*
>A name with enormous energy and charm, that of the greatest hero of Irish myth, Finn MacCool. Other related cool starbaby names: **FLYNN** (Elle Macpherson), **FINNIGAN** (Eric McCormack), **FINLAY** (Sadie Frost) and **FINLEY** (Chris O'Donnell), not to mention Julia Robert's phabulous Phinnaeus.

GAIA *Emma Thompson*
>Inspiration for this unusual name was found in classical mythology, Gaia being the primeval goddess of the earth.

GIGI CLEMENTINE *Cynthia Rowley*
>See Coco.

GOD'ISS LOVE   *Little Mo*

Some parents – especially those of the American
Rapper persuasion – are moving beyond such religious/
spiritual names as Genesis, Trinity, Miracle, Heaven and
Nevaeh (Heaven spelled backwards) to more extreme
examples like this and Praise Mary (DNX).

HARLOW   *Patricia Arquette*

Rather than go the first-name route to vintage
Hollywood glamour, à la Ava and Audrey, this actress
used the surname of the epitome of 1930s sex appeal,
Jean Harlow.

HOMER   *Bill Murray/Richard Gere & Carey Lowell/Anne Heche*

Yes, Homer, one of the old-fangled names sidling back
into favour, often used to honour an ancestor.

HONOR   *Tilda Swinton*

A renewed search for traditional moral values has
prompted a revival of interest in 'virtue' names –
Honor, Hope, Faith, Grace, Charity, Prudence, et al.

IRIS   *Sadie Frost & Jude Law*

Floral names like Rose and Lily are spreading like
wildflowers, but these cool babynamers dared to pick a
bloom that has been long out of fashion and so make it
sound new again.

ISADORA   *Björk & Matthew Barney*

Lagging far behind cousin Isabella in popularity, perhaps
due to too close a tie with tragic modern dancer
Isadora Duncan or to fusty male version Isidore, Isadora
is, we think, as did this quirky couple, worthy of revival.

JASPER   *Don Johnson*

An ideal choice that has both backbone and style,
a combination difficult to find in a boy's name, with
an artistic association with painter Jasper Johns.

JAYA   *Laura Dern & Ben Harper*

This exotic name of a Buddhist goddess makes an
interesting alternative to the trendy Maya.

JAZ ELLE   *Steffi Graf & André Agassi*

The athletic energy of this championship couple is
reflected in their daughter's name. Jaz – often used as a
nickname for Jasmine and thus reflecting that trend –
projects what can only be called a jazzy image.

KAL-EL   *Nicholas Cage*

The birth name of Superman is unlikely to impart any
superhuman qualities to any mortal boy, and thus not as
cool as it thinks it is.

KEEN   *Mark Ruffulo*

Sharp.

KINGSTON   *Gwen Stefani & Gavin Rossdale*

This Jamaican place name and elegant British surname
also boasts the more regal yet user-friendly short form,
King.

KYD MILLER   *Tea Leoni & David Duchovny*

Fortunately, this kyd is known by his middle name.

LAIRD   *Sharon Stone*

This celebrity mum chose to make her son the Laird of the manor, with a name that has a pleasantly distinctive Scottish burr.

LENNON   *Patsy Kensit & Liam Gallagher*

Naming a child after your cultural or other hero gives him two cool advantages: a name with real meaning and a positive image to reach towards. Rocker Zakk Wylde chose Hendrix as his son's musical hero name.

LIBERTY   *Ryan Giggs*

A staunch, principled 'word' name chosen by this footballer.

LILLIAN AMANDA   ·   *Baz Luhrmann & Catherine Martin*

Names usually take four generations to become cool again, and Lillian – last stylish a century ago – qualifies on that score, sounding fresher today than the more popular Lily.

LOLA   *Annie Lennox/Chris Rock/Denise Richards & Charlie Sheen/Carnie Wilson/Lucy Pargeter/Sara Cox*

Madonna's use of Lola as her daughter Lourdes' nickname brought Lola from the smoky back room to centre stage in terms of style. (Other lilting double-'l' names: **LILA** (Kate Moss) and **LILY** (Kate Beckinsale, Chris O'Donnell, Kathy Ireland and Johnny Depp).

LUCA   *Colin Firth*

The Italian roots of their mother are reflected in the names of the two Firth boys – Luca and Mateo – both of them easy to pronounce and assimilate.

MADDOX *Angelina Jolie*

It's a surname-name with a twist, more offbeat than the upstanding Coopers and Walkers, and sexier too, thanks to the final '*x*'.

MAGNUS *Will Ferrell*

A powerful name with a magisterial quality, one of the newly unearthed ancient history artifacts – it dates back to Charlemagne, called Carolus Magnus, or Charles the Great.

MASON *Kelsey Grammar*

Fine for a boy, cooler for Frasier Crane's little girl.

MATILDA *Michelle Williams & Heath Ledger*

So-far-out-it's-in possibility with Aussie connections, might be slated for a comeback after being chosen by this high-profile couple.

MATTEO BRAVERY *Benjamin Bratt*

Attractively energetic Latin version of the classic Matthew, combined with a new-fangled virtue word. Colin Firth is Dad to a Mateo.

MILLER *Stella McCartney*

An up-and-coming new occupational surname choice.

MILO *Ricki Lake/Liv Tyler/ Camryn Manheim*
Jaunty.

MINGUS *Helena Christensen*

Not easy to pull off – recommended for dedicated jazz fans and supermodels only.

MOSES   *Gwyneth Paltrow & Chris Martin*

Venerable, white-bearded Old Testament name brought into the 21st century as Apple's brother.

NAVY   *Nivea & Terius Nash*

When R&B singer Nivea chose her daughter's name, she thought of it in terms of the colour and not the sea-going armed service.

OSCAR   *Hugh Jackman*

This cheerful Victorian favourite is having a definite revival among stylish parents on both sides of the Atlantic.

PHOENIX CHI   *Mel B*

Posh isn't the only Spice Girl with baby-naming talent. Phoenix is not only a trendy place name, but has mythological overtones symbolizing immortality.

PILOT INSPEKTOR   *Jason Lee*

This film star took the trend of word/profession names and doubled it, adding a spelling variant for good measure.

PIPER   *Gillian Anderson/Brian De Palma/Cuba Godding Jr.*

High energy and music.

POPPY HONEY   *Jamie Oliver*

Poppy is cool, Honey a little gooey; when combined they sound more like recipe ingredients than a name.

PRESLEY *Cindy Crawford*

Not as in-your-face cool as Elvis but truer to the spirit of hip, Crawford is not the first to use this name: American country singer Tanya Tucker gave it to her daughter.

RACER, REBEL, ROCKET, ROGUE *Robert Rodriguez*

This American film director *(Spy Kids, Once Upon a Time in Mexico)* is definitely of the school that believes in giving kids names they have to live up to – or live down.

RAFFERTY *Sadie Frost & Jude Law*

One of the coolest of the Irish surnames, with a raffish quality all its own.

RIPLEY *Thandie Newton*

A powerful, androgynous name, perhaps inspired by the commanding character played by Sigourney Weaver in the *Alien* movies.

ROAN *Sharon Stone*

A strong, red-haired Irish name.

ROCCO *Madonna*

The power of Madonna: making this muscle-bound he-man name cool outside of Sicily.

ROMEO *Victoria Adams & David Beckham/Jon Bon Jovi*

Romeo, Romeo, where fore art thou? Thou art a previously quasi-taboo, overly dramatic Shakespearean exclusive that's now been legitimized as a baby name possibility by Posh and Becks, who chose it for their second son, a path followed by rocker Bon Jovi.

ROWAN   *Brooke Sheilds*

This friendly Irish surname was almost unheard of as a girl's name before Brooke Shields made the gender switch; now it shows lots of potential as a likeable, unisex, Gaelic choice.

SACHA/SASHA   *Kate Capshaw & Stephen Spielberg / Vanessa Williams / Jerry Seinfeld*

This Russian male nickname has really taken off for girls, given a boost by sensational Olympic skater, Sasha Cohen.

SAILOR   *Christie Brinkley*

A name with personal meaning for Brinkley and her husband – always the foundation of a truly cool choice – that's inspired other occupation names like **GARDENER** and **BAKER**

SCARLET/SCARLETT   *Sylvester Stallone*

Actress Scarlett Johannson has done more for this rosy name than Scarlett O'Hara ever did, making the name red hot.

SHEPHERD   *Jerry Seinfeld*

Occupational surname with a pleasant, pastoral feel.

SHILOH NOUVEL   *Angelina Jolie & Brad Pitt*

Despite rampant rumours that they were going to pick an African name, this high profile couple opted for a Biblical place name, meaning 'God's gift' or 'peaceful one' in Hebrew, for their daughter. Middle name Nouvel, French for 'new', is also the surname of one of Pitt's favourite architects.

STELLA   *Melanie Griffith and Antonio Banderas / Elisabeth Shue /*
         Dave Matthews / Dan Ackroyd / Jennifer Grey / Peri Gilpin
         It seems all the names containing the letters 'ella' are
         magic in celebrity land these days, which includes Ella
         itself, and the more Latinate extensions Stella, Bella,
         Isabella and Gabriella, all of which have an alluring,
         rhythmic sound.

STELLAN   *Jennifer Connelly & Paul Bethany*
         An interesting Scandanavian import – both strong and
         somewhat exotic.

SURI   *Katie Holmes & Tom Cruise*
         This obscure multi-cultural name hit the headlines as
         the daughter of TomKat, provoking heated debate
         among name experts as to its actual meaning.

TALLULAH   *Demi Moore & Bruce Willis / Simon LeBon*
         The Willises launched the cool starbaby name concept
         when they chose **SCOUT** and **RUMER** as well as the
         more user-friendly Tallulah for their girls.

TRUE   *Forest Whitaker / Joley Fisher*
         Inspirational, aspirational word name that works
         particularly well as a middle name. Joely Fisher named
         her daughter True Harlow: a real trend-blend.

VIOLET   *Jennifer Garner & Ben Affleck*
         Soft and sweet but not shrinking, Victorian Violet, one
         of the prettiest of colour and flower names, chosen by
         these high-profile parents, has begun what is certain to
         be a rapid rise to popularity.

WALLIS   *Anthony Edwards*

    Rescued from single-owner purgatory (via the Duchess of Windsor) and given new life.

WILLOW   *Will Smith & Jada Pinkett Smith*

    A graceful nature application that also relates to Dad's name (as son Jaden's does to Mum's).

XAVIER   *Tilda Swinton*

    This long neglected saint's name is being reassessed, what with the current enthusiasm for names with exes and zee sounds.

ZAHARA   *Angelina Jolie*

    Delicate but strong multi-cultural name bestowed on her Ethiopian-born daughter by Angelina Jolie; Chris Rock used the abbreviated Zahra for his.

ZOLA   *Eddie Murphy*

    As seductive as Lola, but with a distinctive, literary twist.

Sahteene
Supermodel Baby Names

I t's not enough that they're 19-year-old skinny, gorgeous, world-revered millionaires. They've got to have all that and babies, too — and not just ordinary babies, but babies with incredibly cool names. Here is the current crop of supermodel baby names:

AMAEL (boy)	Audrey Marnay
ARPAD FLYNN	Elle Macpherson
ARTHUR ELWOOD	Jasmine Guinness
AUDEN (boy)	Amber Valletta
AURELIUS CY	Elle Macpherson
CASPAR, CLEMENTINE	Claudia Schiffer
CECILY	Stella Tennant
DYLAN BLUE (girl)	Carolyn Murphy
ELLA	Lucie de la Falaise
ELLA RAE	Rhea Durham
FRANKIE-JEAN	Donna D'Errico
HAMZAH (boy)	Yasmin Warsame
HENRY	Heidi Klum
IRIS	Stella Tennant
JASMINE	Stella Tennant
KAIA JORDAN	Cindy Crawford
LENI	Heidi Klum
LILA GRACE	Kate Moss
LUCAS	Cecilia Chancellor / Natalia Vodianova
MARCEL	Stella Tennant
MINGUS LUCIEN	Helena Christensen
NIMA (boy)	Trish Goff
ORSON	Lucie de la Falaise
PRESLEY (boy)	Cindy Crawford
SAFFRON SAHARA	Yasmin leBon
SAHTEENE (girl)	Laetitia Costa
SYCLAR PIM (girl)	Frédérique van der Wal
SKYLA LILY LAKE	Liberty Ross
SCHUL	Liya Kebede
TALLULAH PINE	Yasmin leBon
TOBY COLE (girl)	Emme
WILLIAM DAKOTA	Angela Lindvall
YANNICK FAUSTO	Daniel Pestova

Edmund
British Royal Names

When the newest British royal baby was born a month early, the world held its breath praying for her health … and anticipating her name. The playful Daisy was suggested as a possibility, but the final choice, Louise, was a royal standard. Cool? Marginally, in a stodgy kind of way. Beatrix and Eugenie were hands-down cooler choices, and so was Zara in its day.

Still, combing the royal rosters of England and Scotland, from the Saxons to the present day, produces many interesting options. This list includes not only the names of ancient kings and queens, but those of present-day little lords and ladies.

Girls

ADELA	EUPHEMIA	
ADELIZA	EUSTACIA	
AFRIKA	FEODORE	
AGATHA	FRANCES	
AGNES	IDA	
ALBERTA	JACQUETTA	
ALESIA	MATILDA	
AMABEL	MAUD	
AMICE	MAY	
ARABELLA	MURIEL	
AUGUSTA	OLGA	
AVELINE	SAVANNAH	
BENEDIKTE	SIBYLLA	
BETHOC	URSULA	
BLANCHE		
CECILY		
CLAUDINE		
CONSTANCE		
CORDELIA		
DONADA		
DOROTHEA		
EDITH		
ELIZA		
ELOISE		
EUGENIE		

Boys

ALBERT
ALFRED
ARCHIBALD
CONSTANTINE
DOFIN
DUFF
DUNGAL
EDGAR
EDMUND
FINLAY
GODWIN
HAMELIN
HAROLD
HUMPHREY
IVOR
LIONEL
LUDOVIC
MALISE
MILO
OCTAVIUS
OTTO
PTOLOMY
ROWAN
THEOBALD
WARWICK

Dashiell
Literary Names

Literary inspiration can arise both from the names of authors and the characters they create. Here are some suggestions coming from the first and last names of writers ranging from Edgar Allen Poe to Zadie Smith, and characters from the pages of books spanning various periods of literary history. But in this category, as always, feel free to think about your own personal favourites.

Authors

ALCOTT

AMIS

ANAÏS

ANGELOU

APHRA

AUDEN

AUGUST

AUSTEN

AYN

BALDWIN

BALLARD

BECKETT

BEHAN

BELLOW

BENET

BLAKE

BLY

BRONTË

BYATT

BYRON

CAIN

CARSON

CARVER

CHANDLER

CHEEVER

CONRAD

COOPER

CRANE

DANTE

DASHIELL

DIDION

DJUNADYLAN

ELIOT

ELLISON

EMERSON

EUDORA

FITZGERALD

FLANNERY

FORSTER

FROST

GALWAY

GIDE

GLASGOW

HADLEY

HAMMETT

HARPER

HART

HARTE

HEMINGWAY

HUGO

ISHMAEL

JARRELL

JERZY

JESSAMYN

JULES

KEATS

KEROUAC

KESEY

LAFCADIO

LALITA

LANGSTON

LARDNER

LE CARRÉ	ROALD
LONDON	ROTH
LOWELL	RUMER
MALLARMÉ	SALINGER
MAYA	SAROYAN
MCEWAN	SHAW
MEHTA	TENNESSEE
MILAN	TENNYSON
MILLAY	THACKERAY
MORRISON	THEROUX
MOSS	THISBE
MUNRO	THOREAU
NERUDA	THURBER
NIN	TRUMAN
NORRIS	TWAIN
O'CASEY	VIDAL
PAZ	WALKER
PLATO	WILLA
PO	YEATS
POE	ZADIE
RALEIGH	ZANE
RHYS	ZOLA
RING	ZORA

Characters

FEMALE

ALABAMA	*Save Me the Waltz*	Zelda Fitzgerald
ALHAMBRA	*The Accidental*	Ali Smith
AMARYLLIS	*Back to Methuselah*	George Bernard Shaw
AMORET	*The Faerie Queen*	Edmund Spenser
ANTONIA	*My Antonia*	Willa Cather
ARABELLA	*The Pickwick Papers*	Charles Dickens
ARIADNE	*Heartbreak House*	George Bernard Shaw
AURORA	*Terms of Endearment*	Larry McMurtry
BATHSHEBA	*Far From the Madding Crowd*	Thomas Hardy
BRETT	*The Sun Also Rises*	Ernest Hemingway
BRIANA	*The Faerie Queen*	Edmund Spenser
BRIONY	*Atonement*	Ian McEwan
CANDIDA	*Candida*	George Bernard Shaw
CATALINA	*The High Road*	Edna O'Brien
CATRIONA	*Catriona*	Robert Louis Stevenson
CHARITY	*Martin Chuzzlewitt*	Charles Dickens
CHARMIAN	*Antony and Cleopatra*	William Shakespeare
CLARICE	*The Silence of the Lambs*	Thomas Harris

CLARISSA	*Mrs Dalloway*	Virginia Woolf
CLEA	*Alexandria Quartet*	Lawrence Durrell
CRESSIDA	*Troilus and Cressida*	William Shakespeare
CYANE	*Metamorphoses*	Ovid
DAHLIA	*Carry On, Jeeves*	P. G. Wodehouse
DAISY	*The Great Gatsby*	F. Scott Fitzgerald
DENVER	*Beloved*	Toni Morrison
DESDEMONA	*Othello*	William Shakespeare
DOMENICA	*Unconditional Surrender*	Evelyn Waugh
EMMA	*Emma*	Jane Austen
ESMÉ	*For Esmé – With Love and Squalor*	JD Salinger
EVANGELINE	*Evangeline*	Henry Wadsworth Longfellow
FAUNIA	*The Human Stain*	Philip Roth
FEATHER	*Bad Boy Brawly Brown*	Walter Mosley
FLEUR	*The Forsyte Saga*	John Galsworthy
GINEVRA	*Villette*	Charlotte Brontë
GUINEVERE	*Le Morte D'Arthur*	Sir Thomas Malory
HANA	*The English Patient*	Michael Ondaatje
HAYDÉE	*The Count of Monte Cristo*	Alexandre Dumas
HONORA	*Sea Glass*	Anita Shreve
HONORIA	*Bleak House* and *Babylon Revisited*	Charles Dickens F. Scott Fitzgerald

HYACINTH	*The Princess Casamassima*	Henry James
ISADORA	*Fear of Flying*	Erica Jong
ISOLDE	*Tristan and Isolde*	
JACY	*The Last Picture Show*	Larry McMurtry
JADINE	*Tar Baby*	Toni Morrison
JULIET	*Romeo and Juliet*	William Shakespeare
JUNO	*Juno and the Paycock*	Sean O'Casey
KIKI	*On Beauty*	Zadie Smith
KINSEY	*A is for Alibi*, etc.	Sue Grafton
LOLITA	*Lolita*	Vladimir Nabokov
MAISIE	*What Maisie Knew*	Henry James
MALTA	*Bleak House*	Charles Dickens
MAMIE	*The Ambassadors*	Henry James
MARIGOLD	*Quartet in Autumn*	Barbara Pym
MARIN	*A Book of Common Prayer*	Joan Didion
MELANCTHA	*Three Lives*	Gertrude Stein
NARCISSA	*Sartoris*	William Faulkner
NENNA	*Offshore*	Penelope Fitzgerald
NERISSA	*The Merchant of Venice*	William Shakespeare
NINETTA	*Nicholas Nickleby*	Charles Dickens
NIOBE	*Metamorphoses*	Ovid
NOKOMIS	*Hiawatha*	Henry Wadsworth Longfellow

ORLEANNA	*The Poisonwood Bible*	Barbara Kingsolver
PANSY	*The Portrait of a Lady*	Henry James
PECOLA	*The Bluest Eye*	Toni Morrison
PEYTON	*Lie Down in Darkness*	William Styron
PILAR	*For Whom the Bell Tolls*	Ernest Hemingway
PLEASANT	*Our Mutual Friend*	Charles Dickens
PORTIA	*The Merchant of Venice*	William Shakespeare
PRAIRIE	*Vineland*	Thomas Pynchon
RAIN	*The Sandcastle*	Iris Murdoch
RIMA	*Green Mansions*	William H. Hudson
ROMOLA	*Romola*	George Eliot
ROSAMOND	*Middlemarch*	George Eliot
SABRA	*Cimarron*	Edna Ferber
SCARLETT	*Gone With the Wind*	Margaret Mitchell
SCOUT	*To Kill a Mockingbird*	Harper Lee
SETHE	*Beloved*	Toni Morrison
SHEBA	*Notes on a Scandal*	Zoe Heller
SIDDA/ SIDDALEE	*Divine Secrets of the Ya-Ya Sisterhood*	Rebecca Wells
STELLA	*A Streetcar Named Desire*	Tennessee Williams
SULA	*Sula*	Toni Morrison
TAMORA	*Titus Andronicus*	William Shakespeare
TAMSIN	*A Few Green Leaves*	Barbara Pym

TEMPLE	*Sanctuary*	William Faulkner
UNDINE	*The Custom of the Country*	Edith Wharton
VELVET	*National Velvet*	Enid Bagnold
VERENA	*The Bostonians*	Henry James
VIDA	*Vida*	Marge Piercy
VIVI	*Divine Secrets of the Ya-Ya Sisterhood*	Rebecca Wells
VIVIETTE	*Two on a Tower*	Thomas Hardy
ZORA	*On Beauty*	Zadie Smith
ZULEIKA	*Zuleika Dobson*	Max Beerbohm

MALE

AMORY	*This Side of Paradise*	F. Scott Fitzgerald
ARCHER	*The Age of Innocence*	Edith Wharton
ATTICUS	*To Kill a Mockingbird*	Harper Lee
AURIC	*Goldfinger*	Ian Fleming
AXEL	*Victory*	Joseph Conrad
BARLEY	*The Russia House*	John Le Carré
BARNABY	*Barnaby Rudge*	Charles Dickens
BEALE	*What Maisie Knew*	Henry James
BENVOLIO	*Romeo and Juliet*	William Shakespeare
BRICK	*Cat on a Hot Tin Roof*	Tennessee Williams
BROM	*The Legend of Sleepy Hollow*	Washington Irving
CASPAR	*Portrait of a Lady*	Henry James

CATO	*Henry and Cato*	Iris Murdoch
CHANCE	*Being There*	Jerzy Kosinski
CLEMENT	*Return of the Native*	Thomas Hardy
CLEON	*Pericles*	William Shakespeare
CODY	*Visions of Cody*	Jack Kerouac
CORIN	*As You Like It*	William Shakespeare
DARCY (surname)	*Pride and Prejudice*	Jane Austen
DARL	*As I Lay Dying*	William Faulkner
DORIAN	*The Picture of Dorian Gray*	Oscar Wilde
FENNO	*Three Junes*	Julia Glass
FITZWILLIAM	*Pride and Prejudice*	Jane Austen
GUITAR	*Song of Solomon*	Toni Morrison
GULLIVER	*Gulliver's Travels*	Jonathan Swift
HEATHCLIFF	*Wuthering Heights*	Emily Brontë
HIERONYMOUS	*City of Bones*	Michael Connelly
HOLDEN	*The Catcher in the Rye*	J D Salinger
ISHMAEL	*Moby Dick*	Herman Melville
JAPHY	*Dharma Bums*	Jack Kerouac
JARVIS	*A Tale of Two Cities*	Charles Dickens
JASPER	*The Pathfinder*	James Fenimore Cooper
JOLYON	*The Forsyte Saga*	John Galsworthy
JUDE	*Jude the Obscure*	Thomas Hardy
LAIRD	*In the Gloaming*	Alice Elliot Dark

LEMUEL	*Gulliver's Travels*	Jonathan Swift
LEVI	*On Beauty*	Zadie Smith
LOCH	*The Golden Apples*	Eudora Welty
MACON	*Song of Solomon* and *The Accidental Tourist*	Toni Morrison Anne Tyler
MAGNUS	*The Accidental*	Ali Smith
MARIUS	*Les Misérables*	Victor Hugo
MELCHIOR	*Brideshead Revisited*	Evelyn Waugh
MILO	*Catch-22*	Joseph Heller
MOR	*The Sandcastle*	Iris Murdoch
NEWLAND	*The Age of Innocence*	Edith Wharton
ORLANDO	*Orlando*	Virginia Woolf
PRAXIS	*Praxis*	Fay Weldon
QUEBEC	*Bleak House*	Charles Dickens
QUILLEN	*Sea Glass*	Anita Shreve
QUINTAS	*Titus Andronicus*	William Shakespeare
RHETT	*Gone With the Wind*	Margaret Mitchell
RILEY	*The Grass Harp*	Truman Capote
ROARK (surname)	*The Fountainhead*	Ayn Rand
RODION	*Crime and Punishment*	Fyodor Dostoevsky
ROMEO	*Romeo and Juliet*	William Shakespeare
RUFUS	*A Death in the Family*	James Agee
SANTIAGO	*The Old Man and the Sea*	Ernest Hemingway
SAWYER (surname)	*The Adventures of Tom Sawyer*	Mark Twain

SEBASTIAN	*Brideshead Revisited*	Evelyn Waugh
SENECA	*Babbitt*	Sinclair Lewis
SEPTIMUS	*The Mystery of Edwin Drood*	Charles Dickens
SHANE	*Shane*	Jack Warner Schaefer
SILAS	*Silas Marner*	George Eliot
TAFT	*End Zone*	Don DeLillo
TRISTAN	*Tristan and Isolde*	
TRISTRAM	*Tristram Shandy*	Laurence Sterne
UTAH	*Under Milkwood*	D. M. Thomas
VERNON	*Vernon God Little*	DBC Pierre
VIVALDO	*Another Country*	James Baldwin
WOLF	*The Sea Wolf*	Jack London
YANCEY	*Cimarron*	Edna Ferber
ZOOEY	*Franny and Zooey*	JD Salinger

And don't forget two of the coolest of all:

FABLE

STORY